1985

IF YOU'RE MAD, SPIT!

And Other Aids to Coping

IF YOU'RE MAD, SPIT!

And Other Aids to Coping

Ben F. Mortensen

Brigham Young University Press

Library of Congress Cataloging in Publication Data
Mortensen, Ben F   1928–
  If you're mad, spit!

  Includes bibliographies.
  1. Counseling. I. Title.
BF637.C6M64   158'.1   77-22796
ISBN 0-8425-0802-3

78 2M 34073

Dedicated to my family—Rene, Steve, Marilyn, Michele, Dick, Matt, Jeanette, Pam, Cheryl, Stephanie, and Shanda.

Contents

Preface

This how-to handbook was written over a period of twenty years, the result of my experiences as a psychologist working in various settings. It represents some of the techniques I have found most useful in helping people overcome their emotional problems, but it is by no means the last word in this rapidly expanding field of counseling. No one knows better than I that all the answers are not in yet, for I have found throughout my career that I have failed to solve people's problems more often than I have succeeded, with a ratio of about 40 percent success to 60 percent failure—about par for most counselors in the field. Part of this dilemma is a lack of effective tools for treating disturbed people. The biggest difficulty, however, is motivating people to change. Time and again I have heard individuals say, "The cure is worse than the disease; I'll keep the problem," or words to that effect.

The solution to this problem lies in research. Counselors must be willing to spend the time and effort necessary to develop better motivational techniques. But the greatest challenge for counselors will continue to be found in the preventive area. I have no doubt that future improvement in our counseling-success ratio will depend heavily on our ability to develop better prevention skills. To do this, we must of necessity be forced to start at the very beginning with the home and family.

I hope these essays will be of assistance to everyone who would like to become a counselor in the difficult but rewarding task of helping conflicted people help themselves.

How to Be an Effective Counselor

Certain attitudes are essential to your becoming an effective counselor. First of all, you must genuinely like people and be able to regard them acceptingly, being on guard against tendencies to sit in judgment and against using your own personal standards as a guide. Counselors in the past have tried to direct and control human behavior through a moralizing directiveness; they have told people what to do and have threatened them with dire predictions if they did not do it. Unfortunately, direct advice-giving procedures, emotional exhortations, and implied threats simply do not work toward long-range changes in the life styles of most people. Telling human beings what they should do and threatening or punishing them if they don't do it generally fail to make any significant changes in their behavior. Abundant evidence, however, shows that positive changes in behavior can be effected if these changes are permitted to grow out of the following conditions:

- An emphasis on personal growth instead of on personal problems.
- A sensitivity to the emotional feelings of the counselee rather than an emphasis on the counselor's intellectualized attitudes.
- An understanding of the immediate situation as it affects the counselee's behavior and a focusing of the counseling on that.
- A recognition of the counselor–counselee relationship as a mutual growth experience.

Only that individual who is strong and secure enough to resist the love of authority will be able to forego the ego-bolstering desire to be a self-appointed straightener-outer, a righter of wrongs, or a do-gooder in the lives of his fellowmen. Goethe once wrote, "It is not hard to observe that in this world man feels most free from his own sins and most blameless when he can comfortably expiate the sins of others." (Goethe, 1829.)

The principles of effective interpersonal relations have been known at least since Jesus gave us his Sermon on the Mount. We can do many things to make ourselves more effective counselors and thus be of real value to people. These ways of behaving must incorporate personal humility and faith in the inherent ability of man to exercise his free agency. In everyday language, for everyday application, we can summarize these methods in the following six basic principles of counseling.

1. Develop Self-Control

The principle is this: No man can be effective in controlling the behavior of others until he first has learned to control himself. This implies all the characteristics of maturity and good adjustment. It means that you must constantly survey your own behavior so that your feelings, biases, and prejudices (and you have them) are kept out of your judgments as much as possible. All of us have a tendency to be authoritative in our approach to other people's problems. We like to tell people what to do and how to do it. This is where we must exercise humility and control. A good rule of thumb is: Never give advice unless it's asked for, and then only sparingly and judiciously. You must also be willing to pay the consequent price in anxiety that comes with counseling people who have problems, and you must work out some personal and acceptable ways of relieving your own tensions as they accumulate. Control implies self-knowledge and self-acceptance.

2. Be a Good Listener

The first step in effective listening is to keep quiet. In this regard beware of passive listening; hear what your counselee has to say; keep the listening active. This is where the need for personal humility stands out most clearly. So long as that man has something on his chest, so long as that woman has a problem, they won't listen to you anyway. Consequently you may as well hear them out. You will gain nothing by the argument that will result if you break in before they are ready to listen to you. Once you have learned to listen and can establish rapport and a permissive environment, your counselee will feel safe to talk to you about his or her real problems. A criticizing, self-righteous attitude on your part will cause the person to tell you nothing or at best only what he or she thinks you want to hear, and neither one of you will profit from the experience.

3. Learn to Communicate

Be very sure that your communicant understands clearly the intents and goals of your joint effort. Ask him to tell you how he feels you can best help him.* Then tell him what you feel you can do for him, and also let him know what you can't do for him. If you can't help him, refer him to someone who can. If you feel you can be of service, work together toward the desired end you have both agreed upon. Remember that you as the guiding person have the privilege, but not the right, of assisting him into more effective ways of living. Through your attitude and behavior you must earn his respect and confidence. This mutual understanding, gained at the outset through a thorough and patient explanation, will save you many a headache later in your counseling relationship.

4. Accentuate the Positive

To the extent possible, put yourself in that man's or that woman's position and look at the situation through his or her eyes. In counseling, this is known as empathy, which is simply experiencing the problem with the individual in a completely uncritical manner. Remember, that man or woman will react to you as you appear to be. That individual will regard you in terms of the way you behave; he cannot see behind your behavior into your heart. As a consequence, he will treat you as the kind of person your behavior indicates you to be. You, therefore, must

---

*Wherever the masculine pronoun is used, unless it refers to a specific masculine antecedent, it may represent either the masculine or the feminine.

be able to see beyond your own needs if you are to be effective in helping him. Furthermore, you must believe that he is basically good, that he wants to be a right sort of person, that he will respond to positive treatment, and that he has the potential to achieve his goal. You must, therefore, look for the good in him and, having found it, emphasize this good as a foundation for building. You must learn to separate the sin from the sinner, not to condone the sin but to love the sinner. Then, accentuate his positive behavior as you work to eliminate his negative behavior.

5. Be Understanding

Whether or not we humans have the right to be treated as individuals, we all believe that we do. Therefore, our attitudes and behaviors must take into account our past and present experiences. What a person believes to be true is true for him insofar as his behavior is concerned. Keep in mind that from that woman's point of view, she is an individual with all attendant rights and privileges. Therefore, you must discover what her feelings, desires, needs, and motivations are. Your own inner wants become unimportant. When you can see the situation from the perspective of her feelings and her viewpoint, you can begin to have some hope that you may be of help to her. Until you have achieved this perspective, you simply have no chance at all to be a good counselor. The three most important words in the field of counseling are: *"I understand you."*

6. Keep It Confidential

The principle here again is to be quiet. If you realize that you are a gossip and that you just can't help talking to others about your fellowmen's problems, you had better leave counseling to someone with more maturity.

The success of your counseling often depends on your ability to keep your counselee's problems confidential. This means that you tell *NO ONE* about his problems unless he gives you permission. When it is discovered that you are a "talker," the word gets around, and you will be left wondering why no one comes to you with his problems. Never discuss a person's problems over the telephone in the presence of another. Also be cautious in discussing a person's problem with someone else merely to illustrate a point. Certainly one of your counselees should never be identified to another, and every precaution should be taken to avoid the possibility of identification. You will find that your reputation as a counselor will be based on your ability to keep your communicants' problems confidential.

It becomes apparent that there is a basic necessity for you to be well adjusted if your counseling is to be successful. Furthermore, you must learn certain things and put them into practice if your counseling is to be effective (Hadley, 1958):

- Have an objective rather than a subjective understanding of human behavior.
- Know the general principles of growth and development.
- Know the conditions under which "normal" growth is optimum.
- Understand the laws of learning and those bearing upon the guidance and control of behavior.
- Understand the typical problems a man and woman face and the forms their inefficient resolution of them takes, and have a consequent ability to recognize the symptoms of behavior disorders.
- Understand the principles of adequate personality development.
- Have an insight into the important causes of maladjustment.
- Obtain a skill in the special techniques of interviewing, obtaining case histories, establishing rapport, and counseling.
- Learn the techniques of adapting therapeutic procedures to the unique demands of the individual.
- Know when to be warm and accepting and when to be tough and insistent as the counselee's behavior demands.

Thus, unless a counselor is willing to equip herself or himself with knowledge and is well enough adjusted that he feels no strong compulsion to enhance his own ego, he cannot be of any real help in assisting his fellowmen out of our society's morass of tension and anxiety. When, as a counselor, you develop this insight, you can aid fearful and anxious humans toward increased faith and confidence; you can assist insecure individuals along the path to security; and you can help the embittered man and woman find renewed goodness in their fellowmen. In general you can be of service to your fellow beings in their efforts to increase their sense of personal worth, to feel a part of all mankind, and to find confidence in facing life. You can be effective in guiding today's youth and in helping them to find an adequate, workable philosophy of life based on Judeo-Christian principles. In the absence of this knowledge and this personal integrity, you will probably add to your counselees' confusions and further increase their problems, regardless of how sincere you might be.

References

Goethe, Johann Wolfgang von. *Wilhelm Meisters Wanderjohre.* n.p., 1829.
Hadley, John M. *Clinical and Counseling Psychology.* New York: Knopf, 1958, pp. 565-66.

Suggested Readings

Menninger, Karl. *The Crime of Punishment.* New York: Viking Press, 1969.
Rogers, C. R. *Client-Centered Therapy.* Boston: Houghton Mifflin, 1951.

How to Treat Troubled Teenagers

In working with troubled young people, counselors should master the following six therapeutic principles.

Insight

Plato said, "The unexamined life is not worth living." Only if you have learned to know yourself, to see clearly your areas of competence and strength, and, more importantly, to recognize your insecurities and weaknesses and the reasons for them will you be equipped to deal objectively with a young person's problems. Why? Because in treating disturbed youngsters you will soon become the target for a barrage of negative, hostile, aggressive emotions relating to problems that are difficult for the strongest person to cope with calmly, if at all.

If you have already examined your life and feel reasonably secure and adequate—at least aware of your vulnerable spots—you should then not be disturbed either by a youngster's anger, criticism, and resentment or by his or her need for warmth and closeness. You should know that these feelings are displaced upon you; they are not aroused by you but by events in the boy's or girl's past life. You will then be free to deal constructively with that individual, to become involved in a therapeutic course of action that will reinforce his or her sense of worthwhileness, basic to recovery. If, on the contrary, you have not taken stock of yourself and if you are insecure, you will be blinded by your own inadequate feelings. If you continue to be frightened, unsure, and unaware of why you are so, you will feel threatened by a hostile boy, though his hostility has nothing to do with you; and you will feel rejected by a withdrawn girl, though her isolation is not of your making. Then, understanding neither the youngster's behavior nor your own reactions to it, you will respond defensively, with anger, browbeating, belittling, or standing at a distance, a pathological course of action that will reinforce the youth's poor self-image, generally the cause of his or her problem in the first place.

Know Your Motivations

Answer these questions: Do you honestly want to work with young people who have problems? Do you feel you have the capacity and endurance for it? Are you able to give of yourself, or must you always be on the receiving end? Why do you want to work with troubled youngsters? Were you troubled as a youngster? Are you getting rid of hidden guilt by caring for disturbed young people? Are you rebelling against something or somebody? Unconscious motivations, unrecognized, can defeat your conscious goals.

Know Your Feelings

Answer these questions: What is it that makes you feel inadequate, insecure, or unsure of yourself? How do these negative feelings influence your behavior? Are they realistic feelings, or are you actually more competent and worthwhile than you allow yourself to believe? Do you want to feel differently about yourself, or are you attempting to meet emotional needs by remaining just as you are? Why can't you tolerate a youngster's display of warmth and affection? Why can't you show warmth and affection in return? Why do you feel so threatened? Why do you feel compelled to withdraw from youngsters who seek you out for help? Why do you make it so difficult for a young person to say please or thank you?

Know Your Needs

Answer these questions: Do you require sympathy, protection, and warmth so much that you err by being too sympathetic, too protective, too warm toward a teenager with problems? Or do you fear closeness so much that you err by being indifferent, rejecting, hostile, and cold?

Do you have an excessive need to be liked or to be constantly reassured? Then you may get angry when the young persons you are trying to help are rude, unappreciative, and uncooperative; or you will feel crushed when you think their negative feelings are unjustly directed against you.

Do you cover up feelings of inferiority with an air of superiority? If so, you will probably reject youngsters who have similar feelings, though their real need is to be accepted.

Do you disguise feelings of inadequacy by being dictatorial, laying down the law, demanding unflinching obedience to rules and regulations? If so, you may prevent a young person from getting close to you, and your rigidity will probably stifle his or her emotional growth.

Do you feel the need to be important, liked at any cost, and do you therefore unconsciously keep others dependent upon you? If so, you may discourage a teenager from being independent and from taking responsibility for his own welfare.

Know Your Prejudices

Do you react to a youngster as an individual human being, regardless of race, color, or creed; or do you react with preconceived ideas passed down to you from parents, friends, or whatever source? Do you label a particular young person as a stereotype of a group? Can you justify your prejudices? Or are they derogatory, and do they get in the way of developing a warm relationship?

When you have examined your life, your personal problems will become more manageable, your reactions to troubled youngsters more mature, and your therapeutic efforts more successful.

Should such rigorous self-examination prove difficult, even painful, take comfort from Dr. Harry Stack Sullivan's words: "No one has grave difficulties in living if he has a good grasp on what is happening to him." (Sullivan, 1954.)

Acceptance

A cardinal principle in the treatment of troubled young people is the importance of accepting their maladjustments.

A young person's problems are frequently both a defense against disapproval and a distorted cry for help. If you reject that boy and that girl and their problems, they will feel even more worthless, more intolerably burdened by guilt. Above all else, if you really want to be of help, accept them as important persons, regardless of their levels of performance, and accept their problems as valid, regardless of the difficult behavioral components that make up those problems.

This does not require you to approve of a youngster's unacceptable behavior. On the contrary, once you acknowledge him or her as a person and recognize his problems, you are then free to intervene actively, to modify his neurotic attitudes and conduct. You free yourself to become a catalyst for change. The adolescent, then, because you have accepted him or her, is more likely to accept your therapeutic intervention.

You will not like what a troubled youngster does or says. You will find it difficult to tolerate the various forms his or her problems take. He may pace restlessly up and down, shout obscenities or suicide threats; she may withdraw into dismal isolation, strike out in hostile abandon, or come too close demanding warmth, attention, and affection. Whatever he or she does, each is still a person, with problems every bit as real as physical illness, a human being with great potential buried beneath his or her neurotic, irrational behavior.

Perhaps the first requirement, before you can accept youngsters and their problems, is to accept yourself as a worthwhile human being. Erich Fromm clarified this concept very well in his psychological explanation of the biblical injunction found in Matthew 19:19: "Love thy neighbor as thyself." He interpreted this commandment to mean that, until and unless you learn to "love" (that is, like or respect) yourself, you will never be sufficiently free from your own private biases and touchy spots, your own carefully concealed Achilles's heel, to love (respect or like) your neighbor—in this context, the troubled youngsters you are working with.

When you get to know yourself and have uncovered those

charged areas in which you are most likely to overreact, and when you have learned to change or at least control your reactions, you can accomplish your therapeutic goals, unthreatened by a youth's conduct. You will be able then to handle young people and their misbehaviors objectively and, most importantly, you will be able to love them.

Your acceptance of the teenager as a person will be genuine—not a passive, "I-can-put-up-with-it" tolerance but an active, outgoing acceptance, with no qualifications or strings attached. You will be able to accept differences in these young people, as well as their right to behave differently, to think and feel differently from the way you think and feel. You will be able to show troubled teenagers that you understand and accept their feelings and problems, and at that point they will be free to start making positive changes in themselves.

You will be able to let youngsters reveal their true feelings and to clarify their thinking without forcing on them your own ideas, without directing or controlling them, without retreating to a distance from them. You will be able to let them assume the initiative and begin to modify their own attitudes and behavior. Because you take their despair, their suffering, and their helplessness seriously, you will give them the basic hope that no amount of simple reassurance can possibly foster, and you will leave the essential responsibility for personal change squarely where it belongs—with them.

Through the process of repeated exposure to your appraisal of their worthwhileness, troubled teenagers may begin to perceive themselves as esteemed individuals. With this change in self-concept, youngsters will have an enriched capacity for developing more satisfactory relationships with others. On you, the counselor, more than on anyone else rests the vital task of maintaining the integrity and dignity of young people. The success of this task is based on the realization that troubled teenagers, no matter what form their problems take, are human beings, with many unfortunate life experiences behind them. Your unconditional, positive acceptance of them and their problems will reaffirm their membership in the human race. They too will be able to exclaim: "I am! I have come through! I belong! I am a member of the family of man!" (Sandburg, 1955.)

Trust

Many youngsters become emotionally disturbed because they have never learned to trust themselves or others or even to feel worthy of trust. A husband and wife team of psychologists once described such a person thus: "The dependent and disturbed young person is in a chronic state of not deeply trusting or liking himself. He expects to fail; to look like a fool; to be rejected and belittled. Even when he does something well, he is unable to draw any sound assurance from that fact." (Overstreet and Overstreet, 1954.)

Because a youngster does not trust others and has not experienced trust from them, he feels cut off from his surroundings, doesn't see his environment realistically, can't make contact, feels fearfully alone. This type of young person generally is inconsistent; he overreacts and is so anxious about his problems that he is unaware of the feelings of others and therefore makes insatiable demands on everyone around him.

One psychiatrist addressing himself to this problem comments simply: "Individuals who are emotionally immature and remain so have not had a sufficiently loving and trusting relationship early in life so that they do not quite dare risk the dangers the outer world seems to present to them." (Binger, 1964.)

Bridging this gap, making up for this tremendous unmet need in early life experiences, this traumatic emotional deprivation, places a three-fold challenge upon the counselor who wants to work with troubled teenagers:

1. To gently and gradually show young persons that they can trust you completely and always, that you accept their realistic needs and will try to meet them.
2. To help them trust themselves and their own feelings, freeing them to grow emotionally as well as intellectually in the trusting relationship that develops between the two of you.
3. To encourage them to trust others—friends, family, and the world through these living-learning situations.

Why Accept This Challenge

As long as a teenager cannot trust himself or you or his environment, his personality will be crippled; he will not be free to relate to people or situations in a healthy fashion; he will remain suspicious, unfulfilled, disturbed. Your task is to offer a loving, trusting relationship, so sincere, so constant, so undemanding, that the youngster will dare to risk trusting himself and you and his world.

How to Achieve This Goal

Building trust is a nebulous, intangible endeavor. Everyone has his or her own way of getting close, of establishing confidence and rapport. Maybe it's nothing more than combing a girl's hair or giving a boy a reassuring pat on the back or, like a nurturing parent, simply making yourself available. Whatever you do, whatever your special way, these suggestions may help:

- Accept youngsters as persons. Whether they are likeable, difficult, or frankly obnoxious, seek them out, show interest in their interests, be aware of their likes and dislikes. Do what they suggest, or explain why you can't in a way that's acceptable to them. Handle their comments, negative or positive, as worthy of consideration, their fears as real.
- Be available to young persons, willing, when time permits, simply to stay with them, making no demands.
- Discuss their needs, fears, problems, and anxieties—not yours.
- Listen to them; encourage them to talk, to tell you how they feel, even if these feelings are negative and hostile.
- Recognize the feelings they express, withholding judgmental and punitive remarks.
- Be consistent; let them learn what to expect. If you are cold to them after being warm and friendly, you will confuse them and will only confirm their feelings of insecurity and worthlessness.
- Reassure them when support is called for.
- Avoid increasing their anxiety. Try not to call attention to their shortcomings, mistakes, and peculiar ways.
- Show them that you genuinely expect them to improve.
- Be patient and forbearing, not forcing or hurrying them into more mature patterns of behavior or new relationships, but letting them test each step they take in small ways over a long period of time.

Through these and other techniques, troubled teenagers will come to develop trust in you, and this is an essential beginning to any therapeutic endeavor.

Listening

The listener "who can go beyond words, who can even go beyond the conscious meanings behind words and who can listen with the 'third ear' for what is unconsciously meant by the speaker, furnishes a climate where the most unexpected disclosures occur that are in a way just short of being miracles on the one hand and the most natural and obvious things in the world on the other hand." (Steere, 1960.)

Once you have cultivated that art of listening to a young person, you have equipped yourself with one of the most therapeutic tools in the entire repertoire of the counseling field. The listening referred to here is therapeutic listening and is certainly not an easy technique to master.

Therapeutic Listening Is Active

In no way should we equate listening with mere passive silence. It should be dynamic and creative. "Although everything is quiet, something stirs." That boy is being helped to formulate and express his thoughts, that girl to verbalize her emotions. "Strain and stress are being released. Listening brings the youngster right to the center of the picture. He or she becomes all-important; we are interested in them [sic], and profoundly conscious of their worth." (Rogers, 1942.)

Therapeutic Listening Implies Involvement

If you care deeply enough to become involved, at the same time preserving objectivity, you will listen attentively, patiently. You will listen, and beyond the words you will hear meanings deep below the consciousness of the individual. Your discernment will encourage the adolescent to talk, help him or her to fresh insights, even spark a determination to change.

But if you listen and nod mechanically, if you are bored and restless when they falter or ramble, your preoccupation will deprive youngsters of the sounding board they need. They will feel

14

choked, stifled, rejected, worthless. A golden opportunity for communication will have been lost.

Therapeutic Listening Requires an Open Mind

If you can withhold judgment and comparison, refrain from praise or blame, and listen with an open mind, you will help teenagers express their real feelings. "A listener extends openness when he accepts the person who is speaking, when he relinquishes all buffing and finishing operations, and takes young people as they come. Such acceptance is no toleration born of indifference but is rather a positive interest in this individual, an interest that is so alive that judgment is withheld." (Steere, 1960.)

But if you classify, label, and judge everything young people say in the light of your personal standards and prejudices, you will hear only what you want to hear, and you will seal yourself off from the real significance of what they are trying to say.

Therapeutic Listening Is Difficult

It is hard to refrain from taking the lead, from directing the conversation into "loaded" areas, from showing off your knowledge, from pressing your opinions and advice, from telling adolescents what you think they mean or what you think they should do. Such behavior is evidence of your own personal insecurities and anxieties, and if you aren't aware of these problems, they will intrude and absorb you so completely that you will be unable to listen to what a young person is saying.

But if you can forget yourself, put aside your problems (or hopefully resolve them), you will be free; the quality of your listening will be free, and the youth you are working with will be free. You will be able to create the favorable climate, so rare but so essential if he is to talk honestly about himself and reach constructive insights.

A counselor who is able to listen, who recognizes the emotional needs and problems of young people, who is genuinely concerned about a young person's distress, and who believes in his ability to help others creates a therapeutic atmosphere. This kindly atmosphere makes troubled teenagers feel that their burden is finally being shared. It is no longer heavy to them. Their

15

feelings of loneliness and anxiety are lessened as they sense acceptance. They are then able to bring their feelings or worries out in the open because the environment you have created makes them feel safe from shame or guilt or fear and safe from criticism or ridicule. Once you make them feel safe, they are well on the road to recovery.

Caring

Victor Hugo once said, "The greatest happiness of life is the conviction that we are loved, loved for ourselves, or rather loved in spite of ourselves."

The most essential quality in a counselor who would like to help troubled teenagers is the capacity to care for them regardless of their problems.

One conflicted youngster is said to have expressed it thus: "I don't care how much you know until I know how much you care."

There are multiple ways in which counselors can meet this now generally recognized challenge:

- If you care about a conflicted boy, you will give of yourself to him—not material things but the important things, such as joy, interest, patience, understanding, knowledge, and humor. All of these positive feelings of love and acceptance you will give him freely, without request.
- If you care about a troubled girl, you will feel responsible for her. This does not mean that you will dominate her or be possessive of her, but rather that you will feel a desire and a readiness to recognize her emotional needs and to respond to her in terms of how she feels, not how you feel or would like her to feel.
- If you care about an unhappy boy, you will feel respect for him. This does not mean that you will make him dependent upon you, but rather that you will allow him to grow and unfold for his own sake. You will let him be his own man. You will help him be aware of his individuality. In essence, you will convey to him the sentiment: "You are worthwhile. I respect you and would like to help you with your problems."
- If you care about an angry girl, you will get to know her. Know

16

more than that she is simply angry. You will come to know why she is anxious and worried, why she feels lonely and guilty. You will develop the understanding that her anger is only a manifestation of something deeper. Then you will realize that she is a suffering girl, not just an angry girl.

■ If you care about an inadequate-feeling boy, you will refrain from mere sympathy. In other words, you will not commiserate with him about the traumatic circumstances of his life because such commiseration precludes requiring him to look at his own participation in those past events. Nor does it require him to look at the useful alternatives that were, indeed, open to him. Nor does it insist that he recognize his reasons for not choosing the health-provoking experiences that were available, which would have helped him feel more adequate. Rather, in your caring for him, you will provide him the opportunity to use and develop his intelligence. This will help him gain useful explanations of his past experiences, particularly those that made him feel insecure and inferior.

Unless you are able to really care for hostile adolescents, to make them feel that they matter to you, that you are available and understanding and concerned about them, that you have warmth and empathy for them and see them as worthwhile human beings with the potential to overcome their problems, until you can see them this way and unless—repeat—you are able to *care*, all the textbook knowledge in the world, all the grade-A classroom performances, all the recently developed scientific techniques will never bring about the changes disturbed youngsters must make to insure their future happiness.

Caring, compassion, tenderness, solace, and the ability and readiness to love can make up the magic key that unlocks the door and frees a young person to return to the warm, wonderful world of healthy interpersonal relationships.

Relating

Young people often develop emotional problems because they have never been able to relate to other people on a mature level. Too often key figures in their early life—an overly harsh or passive father, a dominating or insecure mother—have so warped

17

their opinions of themselves that they have lost their sense of self-worth. Consequently, these young people relate to others, if indeed they do not withdraw altogether, as if they expect everyone to think they are no good.

Helping a youngster relate to others in a healthy fashion, then, is one of the counselor's prime goals. The following are suggestions that can help you help a troubled teenager develop more therapeutic interpersonal relationships.

Be Sensitive to the Kind of Reaction You Call Forth in Others

Ask yourself what there is about you that seems to evoke a particular response from a youngster. What is there about you that makes interpersonal relations easy or difficult? If the latter, how can you change? What emotional satisfactions do you receive from your relationship with disturbed young people?

Recognize That Differences in Behavior Are Inevitable

If a young person reacts differently from you to given situations, there is no reason to condemn him or her. Fears and the right of an adolescent to have them must be recognized. By the same token, if you acknowledge your own right to feel inadequate and frightened in certain situations, you will be better able to accept the adolescent's right to feel as he does even if the circumstances do not warrant his reactions.

Be Consistent and Firm

It is axiomatic that all disturbed youngsters are insecure and uncertain, no matter what their behavior may appear to be on the surface. Therefore, one of the most effective measures in promoting a sense of security is consistency of experience. You can reinforce this consistency every hour, every day:

(a) In routines that help young persons by decreasing the number of decisions they must make and by setting up for them schedules upon which they can depend.

(b) In attitudes that remain consistent and predictable among all persons working with or relating to them.

(c) In limitations that are quietly set up and matter-of-factly enforced.

18

"Tread Softly and Go Far"

There is great wisdom in this old Chinese proverb. Probably the most common mistake in initiating and developing a relationship is due not to a counselor's lack of perception or failure to resolve feelings but to his or her overenthusiastic and impatient efforts to establish a relationship with a troubled teenager. Approaching a boy or girl too quickly, too directly, too closely, and too verbally causes a young person to react with resistance to involvement.

If, on the contrary, you can curb these tactics and approach gradually and quietly, the youngster will feel free to draw closer. The relationship between a young person and an adult must crawl before it can walk; so let it crawl in the sense that its demands on the teenager are few and that the teenager is not expected to live up to the demands of intimate relationships until he or she is ready to initiate them.

Make No Demands

Try instead to draw the young person into some kind of response without at the same time *demanding* a response. The adolescent must be left free to respond because he or she wishes to. This will mean, for a while, one-sided conversations and one-sided interest in the teenager's appearance and almost everything else related to him. This interest should always be sincere and without retaliation by word, posture, gesture, or attitude for his failure to respond.

Reduce Young People's Anxiety

In whatever way they evidence anxiety and a consequent resistance to involvement—in physical or psychological withdrawal, by physical or verbal attack, or through gestures and symbolic belittling—young people can learn, with your help, to reduce their anxiety and to participate in healthy interpersonal relationships.

These four suggestions should prove helpful.

- Help them recognize their anxiety.
- Help them see the immediate situation that causes an increase in their anxiety.

- Help them to describe verbally the interactions that produce an attack of anxiety.
- Help them understand the behavior they employ to relieve their anxiety.

Set a Good Example

Through daily contact with you, disturbed youngsters have an opportunity to relate to an emotionally healthy person. They may well compare the more satisfying interpersonal experience between the two of you with former interpersonal relationships that were devastating to them. In the comparison, they may gain insights as to how their behavior can affect a relationship positively or negatively. Repeated testing of this new understanding occurs until a new behavioral response becomes acceptable to them.

Make Full Use of Group Therapy

You will continously have occasion to observe how young people's ability or inability to relate on a one-to-one basis carries over into their interactions with groups of people. Thus, through the dynamic confrontations that are bound to occur in groups, you will have many opportunities to help teenagers learn how to tolerate and share in healthy group experiences. Group living is inevitable in the family, in a job, and in society; and young people need constant practice in this art.

To be understood, young people must be able to express themselves clearly. To understand others, they must be capable of observing and evaluating behavior. To establish relationships, they must be able to respond and to reach agreements. They must be able to combine all these activities in a continuing exchange of messages. (Ruesch, 1957.)

As disturbed youngsters learn to relate to one another in groups, they will begin to communicate better, express themselves more confidently, appraise each other more realistically, make decisions more deliberately, see their mistakes more clearly, and correct their performances more wisely. The result will be greater improvement in their interpersonal relationships.

How much better life would be if everyone practiced mental

hygiene so that no one would develop emotional problems! But since this is not so, the best thing to do is educate our young people so that they can overcome their personal problems and in turn treat other people in such a way that no one will need psychotherapy.

In an unpublished address the late psychologist Abraham Maslow said:

Let people realize clearly that every time they threaten, humiliate, or hurt someone unnecessarily or dominate or reject another human being, they become forces for the creation of psychopathology, even if small forces. Let them also recognize that every time a person is kind, helpful, decent, warm, democratic, and affectionate, they become a psychotherapeutic force, even though a small one.

References

Binger, C. A. L. *The Encyclopedia of Mental Health.* New York: Franklin Watts, 1964, p. 542.

Fromm, Erich. *The Art of Loving.* New York: Harper Bros., 1956, p. 47.

Hugo, Victor. *Useful Quotations: A Cyclopedia of Quotations.* New York: Grosset and Dunlap, 1936, p. 353.

Maslow, Abraham. Unpublished paper given at Stanford University, 1969.

Overstreet, H., and Overstreet, B. *The Mind Alive.* New York: Norton, 1954, p. 72.

Plato. *Dialogues.* Apologia. Chicago: William Benton, p. 38.

Rogers, Carl R. *Counseling and Psychotherapy.* New York: Houghton Mifflin, 1942, p. 35.

Ruesch, J. "Remarks about Communication in Schizophrenia." Paper presented at the International Congress of Psychiatry, Sept. 1957, Zurich, Switzerland.

Sandburg, Carl. *The Family of Man.* New York: MACO Magazine, 1955, prologue.

Steere, D. V. *On Listening to Another.* New York: Harper Bros., 1960, pp. 1-13.

Sullivan, Harry Stack. *Conceptions of Modern Psychiatry.* New York: Norton, 1954, p. 24.

How to Help Others Be Honest

One of the concepts we try to teach one another in the Forensic Unit (a unit treating public offenders, or the criminal patient) at the Utah State Hospital is honesty. Honesty toward others; honesty with oneself.

Psychological studies of the past have demonstrated that all people are dishonest from time to time in order to gain their own selfish ends. Sometimes individuals will be dishonest to escape discomfort or punishment or to gain something desired of material worth or to acquire some sort of advantage over someone else.

An interesting study of human character by two social scientists (Hartshorne and May, 1940) points out that a positive relationship exists between honesty and intelligence. Certainly one is not born honest or dishonest; these are learned traits. Nor does it follow that because one has lower than average intelligence, he or she will automatically be dishonest. However, inasmuch as deceit offers a means of handling a problem, the less intelligent are more likely to use methods classed as dishonest in solving the various problems they meet in life. The more intelligent are likely to be more able to make certain positive adjustments to their problems without having to resort to deception. By the same token, they may be more clever at deception because of their higher intelligence. Someone once said, "Educate a person without moral or ethical principles and you will make of him but a clever devil."

The study by Hartshorne and May demonstrates that people

who are emotionally unstable have a greater tendency toward dishonesty than those who are emotionally well adjusted. Maladjusted people tend to exaggerate or embellish the truth in an attempt to place themselves in the most favorable light possible. Their own insecurities prompt them to prevaricate because they feel that others would not accept the truth about them. When these individuals lie about someone, it is frequently to feel superior to the person about whom they are lying and to try to pull that person down to their maladjusted level of mental functioning. Jealousy seems to be the prime motivation in this type of situation.

Hartshorne and May (1940) pointed out that no generalized uniform trait that can be labeled *honesty* characterizes any one person in all situations. An individual may lie, cheat, or steal in one situation and be completely without guile in another. For example, a person can be dishonest in a business transaction but very honorable in reporting his income tax. He may speak only the truth about his neighbors but cheat in a game or on a test. Whether a person is honest or dishonest in a given situation usually depends upon how much is at stake for him at that specific point in time.

It seems evident from this study and similar ones that, although everyone practices deception from time to time in one form or another, the more intelligent and better adjusted among us feel less of a need to be deceptive in our daily interpersonal relationships.

Everyone seems to be aware that honesty toward others is a basic law of life. Most people have been taught about the honesty storekeeper Abraham Lincoln practiced when he trudged miles to return a customer's change. Fundamental as is this type of honesty, it can in no way compare in importance to being honest with oneself. Interestingly enough, dishonesty toward others is not a major problem with patients in the Forensic Unit. Honesty with oneself, however, is probably the problem that arises most often with the psychopath. But dishonesty is damaging not only to the criminal; it is profoundly damaging to everyone. Clinical psychologists have discovered that failure in self-honesty is at the root of almost every emotional and mental disturbance. Industrial psychologists know that countless men and women lose jobs and ruin careers because they are poor judges of their own abilities and aptitudes. They simply are not honest with themselves. Marriage counselors have also learned that in every disturbed marriage there is, in both men and women, a vast amount of self-deception. In the Forensic Unit at the Utah State Hospital we see over and over again the havoc created in the lives of patients committed with serious criminal charges because of their failure in the past to be honest with themselves.

The emotional rewards of self-honesty are its most potent dividends. A mature self-knowledge greatly reduces the anxiety with which we humans live. Dr. Carl Rogers (1942) noted in his counseling that people with emotional problems have a low opinion of themselves. But once they are able to experience the counselor's acceptance of them as worthy individuals in spite of their problems, a very positive change takes place. Soon they are admitting not only their faults but their good points as well. From self-acceptance it is only a short step to emotional health.

Thus it is in the Forensic Unit that, as we are able to help patients be honest with themselves, with their emotions, with their communications and human relations, they are able to overcome their negativism and self-hatred. They are able to stop punishing themselves and their families by committing crimes. They are able to accept their own faults and shortcomings as well as their virtues and strong points. As they are able to accept themselves, they are better able to accept other people. Less and less do they feel a need to exploit and manipulate others to gain some unfair advantage.

In his book *The Creative Years* (1959) Reul Howe tells about a young teacher who was put in charge of a class of incorrigible delinquents. One boy in particular, fifteen-year-old Joe, delighted in throwing the class into an uproar. One afternoon in desperation the teacher kept Joe after school and asked him why he delighted in making her life so miserable. For a moment he looked sullenly at her, and then replied, "Because you're such a sucker for it."

"I know I am," she replied. "I've always been afraid of people like you, and yet I would like to do something for you. Wouldn't you like me to take an interest in you and help you?"

To her amazement this little bully broke down and poured out to her the story of his unhappy life, so full of misery, poverty, and loneliness. "Her emotional honesty," Howe says, "called forth the truth from this confused, hostile, and resentful boy." Her power to accept herself with all her fears and weaknesses became her power to accept him. This in turn made it possible for him to accept himself.

In the Forensic Unit we have patients who have been charged with every crime imaginable. Sometimes we find ourselves frightened of our patients because of their potential danger. But as we are able to recognize our fears, to admit them to ourselves and the patients—in short, as we are able to be honest with ourselves about our feelings concerning patients, they are able to be honest with their feelings about us; in turn, we are able to help each other. Sometimes we find staff members who can't be honest about their feelings concerning criminal patients. They usually don't last, finding excuses to move on to a less demanding, more comfortable work setting. Sometimes it is the reverse: patients cannot be honest with themselves, their fellow patients, or the staff. These people soon eliminate themselves from the program in one way or another.

Almost all experts agree that, in a person's search for self-honesty, the greatest danger is the human tendency to castigate oneself. Too many people equate self-honesty with self-condemnation. But genuine self-honesty includes an appraisal of both bad and good. We all need to recognize our faults; we must also recognize our potentialities so that we can develop them.

In this regard one of the worst mistakes people make is to deliberately suppress their true personalities. For example, one young, inadequate-feeling patient never wore her glasses around men even though without them she was almost blind. She also put a severe restraint on her rather sarcastic wit lest she deflate male egos and be unpopular. Finally one day, tired of putting on an act of shyness, innocence, and demureness, she announced, "From now on I'm going to be myself and people can take it or leave it." That one decision not only helped her overcome her inferiority complex but also made her a more interesting and attractive young lady. Shortly thereafter she was asked out on a date and so impressed her escort that six months later he asked her to marry him.

The goal of self-honesty has been summed up by Dr. Carl Rogers (1961) in the phrase, "the open self." Persons who achieve mature self-knowledge and thereby self-honesty are no longer afraid of life—no longer must fight life. These people can now accept all their experiences and feelings, whether of grief or of happiness, of love or of guilt. As they are able to accept and communicate honestly all their emotions and feelings, they are more able to accept all the feelings of others. At this point they are ready to step out of their own self-made psychological dungeons into the bright, warm world of genuine and sincere interpersonal relationships.

No one has summed up honesty better than Shakespeare in his play *Hamlet* (1570), when he has Polonius say, "This above all: to thine own self be true, and it must follow as the night the day, thou can'st not then be false to any man."

References

Hartshorne, Hugh, and May, Mark A. *Studies in Deceit.* In Ogburn and Nimkoff, *Sociology.* New York: Houghton-Mifflin, 1940, p. 181.

Hartshorne, Hugh, and May, Mark A. *Studies in the Organization of Character.* In Ogburn and Nimkoff, *Sociology.* New York: Houghton-Mifflin, 1940, p. 186.

Howe, Reul L. *The Creative Years.* New York: Seabury Press, 1959, p. 21.

Rogers, Carl R. *Counseling and Psychotherapy.* Boston: Houghton-Mifflin, 1942, p. 30.

Rogers, Carl R. *On Becoming a Person.* Boston: Houghton-Mifflin, 1961, p. 21.

Shakespeare, William. *Hamlet.* The Complete Works of William Shakespeare. (New York, 1958), p. 950.

How to Help the Insecure Develop Self-Love

Victor had always been a puzzle to his friends. Few students really had as much right to be pleased with themselves, yet— except on rare occasions—he was shy, withdrawn, and self-critical. He ranked high in his college class but never took pride in it because others were higher. Alone with one or two other close friends, he could be talkative, witty, and delightful, but in most groups he was ill at ease, quiet, and solemn. He was ruggedly handsome, but thought himself tough-looking and disliked his features so much that when he lunched in the cafeteria, he sat with his back to the mirrored wall in order not to see his own face.

Then one day, despondent, depressed, and on the verge of suicide, he decided to see a counselor. After a few months of counseling, he learned to see himself more objectively, as his friends had seen him in college. In short, he learned to like himself, and it simply made everything and everybody look different to him.

If a person such as Victor thinks ill of himself, praise or reassurance is about as useful as sweeping a tide of water back with a broom. He cannot help thinking that everyone finds him worthless, stupid, and ugly, because this is his opinion of himself. Disapproval of oneself is like a radical flaw in the lens of the eye; the shape of all things comes through distorted and wrong.

This seems to be the central problem in the lives of a vast number of people in our society, for the way we have our goals built into us as we grow up contradicts the basic human need to find ourselves acceptable and likeable. "An enemy within, an I who condemns or despises part of me, is an enduring and inescapable foe—compared to whom, the enemies from without are but trifles." (Whitman, 1855.)

Is it not ironic that the animals are so much wiser than we humans in this matter? Not one of them, as far as we know, dislikes its own color or shape, thinks of itself as undesirable, is ashamed of its own feelings and emotions. Only we human beings, with our superior brains, have managed to think of our normal, natural selves as unattractive, unlikeable, inadequate, insecure, and inferior.

Over the decades a great many psychologists have been fascinated by this phenomenon and have studied it both in patients and in groups of normal people. The list of sorrows and disorders they have identified as coming from an inability to accept and like the real self would fill volumes. At one end of the continuum it would include such chronic lesser complaints as anxiety, loneliness, guilt, and psychosomatic symptoms, and at the upper end severe mental illness and suicide. The problem can be simply stated as: disliking oneself because of the conflict between the Super-Self and the Real-Self.

Each individual, as he grows up, acquires from his parents and his everyday experiences a set of notions as to what is expected of him. He forms in the unconscious part of his thinking process (as well as in the conscious part) a picture of the ideal person he ought to be, or the Super-Self. While it is right for parents to give a child a set of values and goals to live by, parents too often unwittingly force upon their child their own unreasonable hopes for an impossibly good, beautiful, talented, intelligent son or daughter. And this causes in the child the beginnings of self-depreciation, for, as psychiatrist Karen Horney points out, it gives the child the feeling that "he is loved for imaginary qualities rather than for his true self"—which, it seems, must therefore be unlovable. (Horney, 1937.)

Of course, as one grows past adolescence he is likely to recognize that this Super-Self is unrealistic, and he learns to settle for the Real-Self. He sees, for example, that he is not going to be another Bach or Beethoven and readjusts his sights to becoming an outstanding college or high-school music teacher. But such

30

sensible reappraisals may go on only at the conscious level; in the larger and more important unconscious area of his thinking the unrealistic and demanding Super-Self is still at work, tormenting him by its superiority to his Real-Self and making him feel lazy, untalented, and generally unworthy of love. And it never lets up, is never satisfied, no matter how hard he tries.

All around us are examples of the damage done by the hidden warfare between the Super-Self and the Real-Self—and of the reconstruction that is possible if those battles are brought to an end. One man struggles to become a doctor, flunks out of medical school, settles for becoming a medical technician, and spends his years ashamed and embittered—all because he followed a course built into him by ambitious parents rather than his own genuine desire to become a playwright. A young woman carries out a very real desire to be a full-time homemaker and mother, at least until her children are in high school, but is plagued by feelings of guilt because she wasted the money her parents spent to send her to college and now fears that she has failed them by not achieving some sort of recognition in her chosen field.

In contrast, some people have their eyes opened by insight into their inner conflicts and become capable of accepting the Real-Self and recapturing the joys of life. For example, a few years ago a gifted young scholar who had grown up in a circle of well-to-do, success-oriented business people fell in love with a socially ambitious girl. Responding primarily to external pressures, he shifted his studies from history to marketing and before he was thirty found himself with a flourishing advertising business, a large, fashionable home, and a swimming pool—plus colitis, migraine headaches, and insomnia.

Because their marriage was floundering, they sought out a psychologist for marriage counseling. Through counseling the psychologist helped them understand the underlying problems that were ruining their lives. One sleepless night this young man found himself thinking of the words of Polonius, "to thine own self be true." (Shakespeare, 1958.) The next day he sold his advertising business and went back to the study of history in graduate school. He eventually accepted a teaching position at half the salary he had been making in the advertising business.

Today he lives happily with his wife in a small apartment near the campus. Their relationship is better than it has ever been, and he no longer has colitis, migraine headaches, or insomnia.

But such external rearrangements of life are not always the key to self-acceptance. Far more often the answer may lie in a reevaluation of the daily events of our lives, without any actual change in those events. Some people complain, when their friends go to a psychologist, that they are spending a lot of money and showing very little change for it. But a good deal of the change is occurring inside, where the patient is learning to feel better about who and what he is and to accept himself as a satisfactory human being. And this acceptance is often all that is necessary. For the way we feel about ourselves makes more difference to our lives than a different job, a higher income, or the good opinion of other people. "Public opinion is a weak tyrant compared with our own private opinion," said Thoreau. "What a man thinks of himself—that is what determines, or rather indicates, his fate." (Thoreau, 1854.)

Is it not curious that some slum children become drug addicts while others, with no greater talent, become successful businessmen? Or that a bad home environment will cause one child to become delinquent or mentally ill—but not his brother or sister? Some people, afflicted with a physical handicap, become embittered, hostile, withdrawn; others go on to become immensely successful human beings—not because of their problems or handicaps but because of the feelings they have that they are valuable people.

In order to survive the difficulties of life and enjoy its rewards, one must not only like the positive things about oneself but also be able to accept and live with all those feelings he or she was taught, as a child, to think of as bad or wicked. That hidden tormentor consists of not only what the Super-Self should be but what it should not be as well. It keeps telling us that a great many of our emotions are terrible and that, not only should we not act them out but we should not even feel them in the first place. Yet most of these forbidden emotions—anger, selfishness, jealousy, and others—are part of our human biological makeup, and although we should learn to control these negative feelings, it is not evil to have them.

On a rainy day when her children are inside screaming and fussing, a harried mother feels that her life would have been more content without them. But this thought fills her with dismay, for it is almost akin to wishing them out of existence. The resulting guilt is so unendurable that she redoubles her efforts to be an ideal mother in order to prove to herself that she really didn't have any bad thoughts after all—and only succeeds in becoming an overprotective mother. Yet the so-called evil thought was a normal thought. The only real evil would have been to neglect or abuse her children.

Every person whose aging parent is going to bequeath him some money looks forward, consciously or unconsciously, to having that money. Yet because it seems like looking forward to the death of the parent, he fears the dreadful thought and tries to pretend that he is incapable of it. This choking back of a real (though not admirable) emotion sometimes has spurious effects. One man inherited his mother's money and invested it so foolishly (though he was ordinarily a sensible, prudent fellow) that he never got to enjoy it at all. This was his way of unconsciously proving that he had never really wanted it in the first place.

To accept one's negative feelings as human and natural does not mean to act upon them; and therein lies all the difference. We are bound to have many such feelings; we were created that way. Our humanity lies in our ability to feel them, understand them, and not carry them into action. But it is the dreaded sense of guilt about having such feelings that damages us and makes us detest ourselves.

Anger, particularly anger directed at someone we love, is very sternly forbidden to children by many parents who call it a "bad" emotion that one mustn't feel. As adults, therefore, many of us feel horribly upset and unworthy when we are angry with a member of our family. To escape the sense of vileness, we thrust the feelings out of sight, and we hope they are out of mind. But real feelings thus dammed up are like a stream that must overflow its banks and burst out across the fields. When a woman chokes back all expressions of her annoyance and anger with her husband, for example, and refuses to admit to herself that she feels them, she is likely to express the dammed-up emotions in other ways. She may lose her capacity to respond lovingly to him, or she may fall into a prolonged depression or develop a severe mental illness. The files of every city coroner's office and every mental hospital are filled with cases of people whose personal lives on the surface seemed devoid of conflict; but the angry or unpleasant feelings they refused to acknowledge erupted suddenly, against themselves, usually in or about the heart.

This is not to extol quarreling and aggressiveness, however. What is valuable is the simple realization that we have the right to our feelings—all of them—kind and angry, loving and hateful, and we must not let ourselves be overwhelmed by our disapproving Super-Self. Merely to admit our negative feelings and to control them is enough to enable us to cast off intolerable and damaging burdens of the heart. When we can recognize these feelings and accept them as part of us, they lose their force and insistence; they no longer become important factors in our life economy. Realistic living demands that we accept ourselves in full, the undesirable as well as the desirable. It helps when we know that the recognition and acceptance of faults tends to obliterate them. Carlyle once said: "The greatest of faults is to be conscious of none." (Carlyle, 1841.)

For instance, when your counselee is mad enough to spit, tell him, "Go ahead and spit! Just be careful *where* you spit." Then, after he has spat, tell him to sit down in close consultation with himself and look into the cause of his anger. The probabilities are that one of his personal sensitivities has been scratched; one of his prideful toes has been stepped on. Many times this kind of recognition alone is enough to reduce the irritating situation to its true proportions and thus allow his sense of humor to come to his rescue.

Some years ago psychologist Abraham Maslow made a fascinating study of a group of the psychologically healthiest people he could find. Describing their feelings about themselves, he wrote, "Our healthy individuals find it possible to accept themselves and their nature, with all their shortcomings and their discrepancies from the ideal image, in a matter-of-fact sort of way, without feeling undue concern." (Maslow, 1954.)

This may sound as if self-acceptance implies a resigned do-nothing attitude (I'm fine the way I am, so there is no need to try to be any better). But this is neither the real meaning of self-acceptance nor the attitude Maslow found in his healthy people. "It would convey the wrong impression to say that they are self-satisfied," he wrote. "What we must say, rather, is that they can take the frailties, imperfections, weaknesses, and all other negative aspects of human nature in the same unquestioning spirit with which they accept all the positive aspects of human nature. This is not a lack of guilt, shame, sadness, anxiety or defensiveness when they do something wrong; it is a lack of inordinate and/or excessive guilt, shame, sadness, anxiety or defensiveness when things do not go their way." It is the difference between the neurotic writer who can never finish anything to his own satisfaction and William Shakespeare, who "never blotted a line"—a man who was ever willing to take a chance on himself.

Perhaps the term *self-acceptance* is too barren for this kind of reasonable liking of self combined with a realistic effort to do one's best. What, then, shall we call it? Self-approval? Self-esteem? Or do we dare to call it by its right name, self-love? Over the centuries that term has usually been a reproach, signifying self-centeredness, selfishness, and vanity. But from time to time a few rare thinkers and writers have gazed deeper, realizing that love of the self is a basic and healthy part of every living thing—the source of the highest morality. Erich Fromm points out that the Bible commands us to "love our neighbors as ourselves," thus using self-love as the primal, essential love upon which all other loves are fashioned. Lacking self-love, the self-despising or self-critical person is not only doubtful of his own worth but cynical about the worth of the rest of mankind. (Fromm, 1956.) As psychiatrist Harry Stack Sullivan has observed, "One can find in others only that which is in the self." (Sullivan, 1964.) Self-love is thus the very source of our own healthy love for other people. And this has been proven by a number of psychological studies showing that those people who, in describing themselves, use favorable terms also tend to describe their fathers, teachers, and other persons in favorable terms, while those who describe themselves critically or have low self-esteem tend to see other people in a poor light.

How shall you go about teaching others to accept and even to love themselves? The following are a few suggestions for those counselors who would like to help the insecure improve their self-image.

First, help them to look within themselves and hide nothing. Before they can learn to stop disapproving of themselves, they must clearly see the hidden motives that are causing them to feel anxious, driven, guilty, or unworthy.

Second, assure them that, having seen them, they must not recoil; they have an inalienable right to have negative feelings as well as positive ones, for both kinds of emotions are a part of all mankind. They must remember that they need not despise or even disapprove of themselves for any negative feelings so long as they control them and do not carry them out destructively toward those they love.

Third, help them learn to compromise with the Super-Self and the Real-Self in themselves. Tell them to welcome the Real-Self and do the best they can to improve it daily.

Fourth, encourage them to love themselves and to be unafraid to let their innate self-love come into being; it is natural, fundamental, healthy. Suggest that they consider the animals—that they sit still and observe a cat washing itself or dozing; that they regard a little child playing. Then encourage them to permit themselves to feel that same, simple, utterly wholesome pleasure in just being themselves.

Fifth, help them to understand that in loving their real selves, they will be better able to love the real selves of other people. Like Walt Whitman, they should be able to say (Whitman, 1855):

"Having pried through the strata, analyzed to a hair, counsel'd with doctors and calculated close, I find no sweeter fat than sticks to my own bones. In all people I see myself, none more and not one a barleycorn less, and the good or bad I say of myself, I say of them also."

References

Carlyle, Thomas. *Heroes and Hero Worship.* 1841.
Fromm, Erich. *The Art of Loving.* New York: Harper & Bros., 1956, p. 47.
Horney, Karen. *The Collected Works of Karen Horney.* New York: Norton, 1937, p. 162.

Maslow, Abraham H. *Motivation and Personality*. New York: Harper & Bros., 1954, pp. 149-80.

Shakespeare, William. *Hamlet*. The Complete Works of William Shakespeare. (New York, 1958), p. 950.

Sullivan, Harry Stack. *The Fusion of Psychiatry and the Social Sciences*. New York: Norton, 1964, p. 204.

Thoreau, Henry David. *Economy*. 1854 (chapter one).

Whitman, Walter. "I Sing the Body Electric." *Leaves of Grass*. 1855.

How to Help the Stressful Live with Tensions

In these days of great scientific discoveries, it is easy enough to assume that all illnesses arise either from germs, viruses, or new growths. While these are responsible for much human suffering, they are not the chief cause of disease today. A far greater number of illnesses arise from an entirely different source. These are the diseases brought on by nervous tension.

It is surprising how many different diseases arise from stress and tension. Among the more common are hypertension or high blood pressure, heart attacks, strokes, peptic ulcers, chronic gastritis, migraine headaches, colitis, bronchial asthma, and chronic skin disorders. Other factors may also enter into some of these conditions, but the emotional impact is most often responsible for the more serious complications.

Psychosomatic diseases involve both the mind and the body. They are not new to the human race; they have been with us for a long time. But today, with most of the serious infections already brought under control, they are becoming more evident. In fact, they account for more deaths than all the infections, accidents, and malignancies added together.

If we look at the term *psychosomatic* we will find that it comes from two Greek words: *psyche,* meaning mind, and *soma,* meaning body. Technically it implies an intimate relationship between psychological phenomena, such as emotional attitudes, and structural changes in the body, i.e., changes in the heart rate, upsets in digestion, and altered brain activity. Since both mental and physical changes take place in the same biological organism, it is only reasonable that they should be but different aspects of the same process. If given sufficient time and stress, emotionally induced alterations in bodily functions may become irreversible and hence permanent.

It has been indicated by the U.S. Public Health Service that some 10 percent of the U.S. population is in need of psychotherapy. It is also estimated that two-thirds of the patients who visit physicians in this country need ongoing psychological counseling along with the usual medical care. The problem of psychosomatic illness therefore requires something more than idle speculation and a mere playing with words; it is a genuine tragedy for those afflicted by it. Surprisingly, the problem is largely preventable.

During the years 1967 to 1970 psychological data were collected on over 1,000 U.S. industrial managers and executives. The following is a report of the five most common psychosomatic illnesses encountered among these people, as well as the personality variables that contributed to their physical problems. The findings of this study will illustrate the essential unity of mind-body relationships and will also demonstrate the ease with which we humans can, and do, become emotionally driven beings.

Hypertension (High Blood Pressure)

The first and most common illness found among executives and managers was *hypertension,* or high blood pressure. Most people are aware that one of the physiological aspects of emotionality is an increase in blood pressure that endures as long as the emotional condition persists. Let's say that a manager or executive develops a rather constant state of anxiety because his performance falls short of the idealistic goals he has set for himself or because a conflict exists between an inner feeling of resentment toward people, for whatever reason, and an external, socialized compulsion to be polite and courteous. Here we see the beginnings of the typical picture of hypertension with the vicious circle that inevitably establishes itself. Let's assume that this manager for some reason lives for awhile in this heightened emotional state. Soon his energy runs out, and he goes to a physician for a checkup. Because of his emotionalized living his blood pressure is elevated, and the hypertension is discovered.

He is usually told to "take it easy," and a sedative is prescribed. But now the knowledge of the hypertension itself becomes an additional source of anxiety, which serves to maintain the heightened blood pressure and often to increase it even further. Anxiety increases, and the circle is complete.

Essential Hypertension

It is important to understand that the hypertension referred to here is the so-called *essential hypertension* for which no organic cause can be discovered. That is, kidneys, liver, and heart appear to be functioning normally, and no evidence of hardening of the arteries (arteriosclerosis) can be found. Also bear in mind that, according to Dr. Edward Weiss, who has studied this illness extensively, 90 percent of all cases of hypertension have their origin in emotional factors. Consequently the findings of this study apply to the overwhelming majority of hypertensive individuals. (Weiss, 1953.)

Just as you and I can develop new habits when we are faced with new situational demands, so also can our circulatory system, under long-continued stress, adapt itself to an altered level of functioning. When such adaptation becomes full-blown, we speak of chronic illness. Under such conditions, our heart and arteries adjust themselves to the emotionalized reactions we make. When this happens, time no longer heals. Rather, the passage of time alone (in the absence of self-understanding or insight on our part) augments the difficulty. This is because emotional living feeds upon itself and increases both in intensity and in scope until physical and emotional breakdown finally occurs. Time and rest by themselves are no help whatsoever in the treatment of chronically emotional (neurotic) behavior.

A reasonable estimate appears to be that some 25 percent of all people beyond age fifty die of emotionally induced hypertension or some complication thereof. Even cancer kills fewer at this age level. Keep in mind again that we are referring to essential hypertension for which no organic cause can be discovered. The high blood pressure arises out of faulty emotional attitudes. These faulty emotional attitudes may be briefly summarized by saying that when a person believes the things he prefers to happen should or must occur, and that it is catastrophic rather than merely irritating when they do not occur, he is being thoroughly irrational. Why? Because reality is what it is, not what we would like it to be. Consequently, the only sane thing to do about an unpleasant situation is either try to change it or, if it is unchangeable, accept it. Getting thoroughly upset—with an increase in blood pressure—about an annoying condition (the same thing as telling ourselves it is a terrible disaster) will not only fail to improve the condition, it may kill us by bringing on a heart attack. This very thing happens every day—a sad commentary on man's rationality! Far too many of us actually seem to court death. That this inadequate, but basically preventable, adjustment to life should annihilate one-quarter of us humans above the age of fifty is hardly evidence for the inherent rationality of man. Since many of these fatalities could have been prevented by more effective training early in life, we face one of the great psychological crimes man commits against himself. Unfortunately, unless intelligent and intensive action is taken, it is also a crime that carries, for too many people, an automatic and irrevocable death penalty.

Hypertensive Personality

To further our understanding, let us look at the hypertensive personality. Managers suffering from this illness seem to present a fairly common personality structure. They often project an exterior of self-control, reserve, courtesy, and warmth. Inwardly, however, they feel a compulsive drive toward perfectionism in their own output. Added to this is an underlying feeling of resentment toward their fellowmen. In a way they try simultaneously both to please and to rebel against life. Unfortunately, the emotional energy aroused by this basic incompatibility expresses itself through their hearts.

Let us not paint this picture too dismally, however. When the hypertensive individual comes for help early in his high-blood-pressure career, counseling can be quite effective. The person is taught how to face life more realistically and to recognize the nature of his inner feelings, even though he does not approve of them. When the difficulty has continued so long that irreversible changes have taken place in the person's circulatory system, much still can be done. While the hypertension as such may not be markedly reduced, the person's attitudes can be improved. The danger that he may worry himself into his grave is therefore strongly decreased.

A brilliant physicist, the head of a nuclear energy research and development department, has suffered from hypertension for the past several years. The man is a study in contrasts, deferential and polite to his peers and superiors but most inconsiderate of his subordinates. Superficially he presents a picture of the quintessence of charm and courtesy, although a somewhat sarcastic tone often underlies his conversation. He obtains sick leave with some regularity and often is forced to ask his assistants to substitute for him in meeting professional obligations because of headaches and general feelings of illness. No organic cause has been discovered to account for his elevated blood pressure; and, since he presents an almost clinical picture of the essential hypertensive personality, one suspects that behind his facade of politeness lurks a rather strong contempt for his fellowmen.

It very much looks as though we shall all have to live with hypertension so long as we continue to train people to adjust to life in ineffective ways. It is equally evident that when we make use of the counseling techniques available, we may stave off the fate that emotional living holds in store for us. Most of us know that insight into our conflicts leads to a reduction of anxiety and hence to a decrease in the physiological commotion anxiety inevitably induces. Fear tends to vanish when faced with fact.

Intelligence alone, however, is not sufficient. Even the brightest person cannot apply what he does not know or what he refuses to admit. It becomes imperative, then, that any person living at this emotional level seek out and ask for the help that is available. When we get really snarled in the ever-tightening net created by our nervous tensions, we cannot work ourselves free without assistance.

Peptic Ulcer

The digestive tract is one of the most common locations of psychosomatic complaints. The gastrointestinal system is often referred to as "the sounding board of the emotions." A great deal of evidence indicates that most gastrointestinal upsets have an emotional base. It is estimated that at least half the people who complain of pain in or about the abdomen are victims of unfortunate emotional adjustments. In fact, there are at least seven million persons in this country who have active peptic ulcers. Nowadays diagnosis is reasonably accurate, and treatment is reasonably effective. Therefore, a sizable number of these stomach sufferers could find a potential cure if they were relieved from the emotional torment of their nervous tensions. It is no uncommon experience for specialists in internal medicine, especially gastric disturbances, to find no demonstrable physical illness in over half their patients. Their pain is a reaction to emotional upset or nervous tension.

Ulcer Personality

Executives and managers who suffer from peptic ulcers show somewhat similar personality characteristics. They are often self-drivers, highly motivated and ambitious, frequently presenting an exterior of great emotional control. Inwardly, the usual picture is one of strong feelings of failure to achieve, hostility, free-floating anxiety, and low self-esteem. They are often energetic workers (although their energy may not be well directed) who drive themselves mercilessly. Consequently, they are often both the envy and the despair of their associates. Nevertheless, these people still feel they are not accomplishing. The anxiety thus developed as a result of a sense of frustration builds internal tensions, and these often become expressed through gastric disturbances. With such people, it is necessary that they strike a more effective balance between their self-imposed goals and their actual achievements. When they are helped to do this, their anxiety often is reduced, with an accompanying decrease in their nervous tensions. Their gastrointestinal system, in turn, becomes freer to perform its normal function unimpeded by the demands of emotional stress.

An insurance executive, known for his drive and charm, spends most of his time and energy running about in tight little circles. He works too hard and plays too hard. Under the influence of alcohol, much of his charm disappears, and he criticizes his colleagues viciously. After a few months on this merry-go-round, his ulcer acts up, and he returns to a diet and a semblance of normal living. He also reports to the company's psy-

44

chologist for counseling sessions. Between these two remedies, he shortly feels able to return to his wheel-spinning and gear-grinding ways. Over the past five years, this cycle has repeated itself some half-dozen times. At present he is hospitalized, and the outlook for him is not good. It is interesting that his last hospitalization occurred within a week after he had been relieved of a considerable segment of his responsibilities. Ironically, he was relieved of these responsibilities because top management felt that his health did not permit him to do the kind of job the insurance company wanted.

In a sense, this man is in the active process of committing suicide. He knows that the pace he sets for himself is too great; yet he is unable to relax to any appreciable extent. His old habits are just too strong. After periods of dieting and counseling, he slows down for a time but gradually picks up speed until shortly he is back in the same old whirl. In his case, neither dieting, medication, surgery, nor counseling have had any enduring effect, and he is a poor insurance risk indeed. The tragedy is that he is a man of unusual basic ability who is so afraid of failure that he will kill himself before he will accept failure. Yet, the very behavior by which he strives to avoid failure will assure him of eventual failure.

In most ulcer cases, symptoms will recur despite close adherence to the usual diet. This recurrence, however, can be prevented if medication and counseling go hand in hand. Both seem to be necessary because the treatment of individual organs within the body is often of no avail. Only when the body is treated as a whole can lasting recovery occur. While symptomatic treatment may relieve, it cannot effect a cure. Taking aspirin for chronic headache is a symptomatic treatment. It is much better, much wiser to go to a counselor and confess all. Whenever disturbed emotions make up an important part of a person's illness, treating just the physical illness will not be completely effective.

Colitis

Colitis is typified by diarrhea or constipation, accompanied by pain and sometimes the presence of mucus in the stools. Occasionally blood may be observed. Colitis is a bodily reaction to tension and stress and is closely related to feelings of anxiety and resentment.

Convincing evidence exists for the emotional background of colitis. In fact, the term was coined a few years ago to represent an illness that was becoming fashionable as the fad for appendicitis was dying out. Most persons who are diagnosed as having colitis suffer from a neurosis quite in the absence of any organic illness.

Colitis Personality

Managers who complain of colitis seem to have deep, almost insatiable needs for affection. They want to be completely loved exactly as they are, without any change on their part. They often seek to obtain this love through humbleness, modesty, and submission. Inwardly, however, they often feel a rather strong resentment and hostility that they are afraid to express openly. Except through their colon, they show little aggressiveness. Their energy level is low, and they seem to need more than the usual amount of sleep.

A young bank manager on the West Coast reported to the company physician with severe cramps in his abdomen, coupled with frequency of bowel movements containing mucus. After treating the initial symptoms, the physician sent the young man to a psychologist. Several consultations revealed that his symptoms coincided with long-standing arguments he would have periodically with his mother concerning the girl to whom he was engaged. Since his mother did not approve of her prospective daughter-in-law, the young man's life in his parental home consisted of an endless series of recriminations and scoldings. He made no attempts to "fight back" but reported that his mother's behavior was a source of intense resentment. After counseling, consisting in part of a discussion aimed at informing him of the mind-body relationships involved, and after the psychologist had consulted with the man's mother, his symptoms ceased—particularly after the mother was able to accept her son's fiancee.

Psychosomatically, it is quite important that the abdominal trouble this young man experienced ceased as soon as an understanding was reached between his mother and him concerning the girl he expected to marry. He had been unable to express outwardly the resentment he felt toward his mother's interference because he had been taught as a youth always to submit to her. "It is an organismic axiom that repressed nervous tension, when it is forbidden a normal outlet, will break out in the malfunctioning of some bodily organ." (Levi, 1967.)

Bronchial Asthma

That the respiratory system is involved in any discussion of psychosomatic disorders should come as no surprise. Most people have felt sensations of pressure in their chests during strong emotional experiences. Their chests have tightened, and they have found difficulty in getting enough air into their lungs. They have probably suspected, on past occasions, that a distinct relationship exists between their nervous tensions and respiratory irritations of one sort or another. Abundant evidence indicates that their suspicions are correct.

In part, asthma involves an allergic reaction to certain substances to which a person is especially sensitive. However, this is not the entire story. Persons have been known to undergo asthmatic attacks at the sight of an artificial rose or a plastic cat. Through the classical conditioning process, first discovered by Pavlov, it is possible to produce such an attack by any reasonable facsimile to the allergen (the substance or object to which the person is especially sensitive). In fact, a case on record tells of a man who suffered from hay fever during the regular ragweed pollen season but only during those seasons when it also happened that his domineering mother-in-law was living in his home.

Asthmatic Personality

Managers who show allergic reactions generally also experience difficulty in making decisions as well as vague feelings of uneasiness and an awful dread of the routine of the day. Such persons also often carry about repressed but intensely frustrating desires. These repressed wishes seem to serve as "trigger mechanisms" to set off an asthmatic attack quite in the absence of the substance to which they are actually allergic.

47

The characteristic personality traits of asthmatics seem to cluster about deep feelings of dependency, a severe lack of self-confidence, and strong anxiety. Such inner feelings can only make for a general life outlook of inadequacy and fear. With such a generalized fear of the things and events in life, it is small wonder that the emotional outlet should appear through so vital a process as respiration. Nothing is psychologically so threatful as the inability to breathe.

A plant manager of an automobile manufacturing firm goes wheezing about his job. As long as his duties are familiar ones (he has some thirty-five years of experience in this particular operation), he pants his way through his work in rather effective fashion. The introduction of unfamiliar methods or the addition of new responsibility changes the picture rapidly. His breathing becomes greatly labored; he flushes, perspires, and makes alternate trips to the dispensary and outside the plant for fresh air. Psychological evaluation of this man indicates low self-confidence, strong uncertainties, and deep fear of anything he does not feel able to handle. Basically, he is a good-natured person and fortunately able to grin at himself and his asthma. In fact, he quite prefers the asthma, a situation he knows well, to the long and deep look into himself that counseling would require. He prefers the familiar and known over the unfamiliar, unknown, and hence threatening. The man is probably right. He has worked out an adjustment of sorts to his ailment; this adjustment functions reasonably well for him, and his case is one best left alone. His good-natured reaction toward his difficulty is contagious, and it is not at all uncommon when a new procedure is being discussed "topside" for senior management to say, "Boy! is old So-and-So going to wheeze over this one!"

Skin Disorders

Emotional tension can and often is reflected in the skin. The most common symptom is excessive perspiration under the arms and on the palms of the hands and the soles of the feet. You may be aware that in heightened emotional states the small blood vessels of the skin contract. This capillary constriction is felt as coldness and clamminess in the extremities. Consequently, the traditional "cold feet" of fear has psychosomatic reality.

Everyone at some time or another has experienced, either in himself or his friends, emotional excitement leading to skin disturbance. This disturbance may have ranged from simple blushing to irritating and lengthy hivelike rashes. Nervous tension can so influence the skin that its entire physiology becomes disturbed.

Skin Disorder Personality

Executives and managers who respond to emotional situations with changes in the condition of their skins also tend to be quite rigid. Consequently, they are easily disturbed by any change in the ordinary routine of their lives. These individuals have tried to crystallize and channelize their living in the hope that they will always have everything under control. Whenever the threat of deviation from this routine occurs, they respond with rather violent internal resistance. Inwardly they are most upset, although they may go along with the change with apparent willingness. However, the internal disturbance often expresses itself through itching rashes or welts on their skin. These people reject innovations and added responsibility because either one will introduce changes in their established life patterns. Remember, they have tried to protect themselves against such change by developing rigid, routinized behavior. Disturbances in the function or appearance of the skin can and will arise out of unreleased emotional tension.

A young lady, manager of design in a large women's clothing manufacturing firm, upon rather slight emotional provocation would blush furiously, and within a period of minutes elongated, raised welts would appear on her forearms. This rash would endure for hours or days, depending upon the intensity of the emotional upset. The attack would be particularly severe if the emotion aroused were one of resentment or hostility, which she experienced when her superior was displeased with her work. If she were not permitted to do things as she wished, within a few minutes she could be seen vigorously scratching her arms although she may have acquiesced smilingly to the change in her patterns and designs. She had been born late in the life of her mother and had grown up under the guidance of parents who were already approaching old age. She became accustomed to a routine existence, in which neither changes nor rebellion were tolerated. She developed the habit of giving in pleasantly, regardless of her feelings; and quite unknown to her, her emotional suppression found outlet in her "hives."

I trust that these examples have demonstrated how nervous tension can affect the human circulatory, digestive, eliminative, and respiratory systems, as well as the condition and appearance of the skin. While these illustrations by no means exhaust a possible listing of psychosomatic processes, they should serve to illustrate my point adequately.

There are at least ten major irrational assumptions that we, as managers of people, unwittingly teach one another. These assumptions seem to create most of our anxieties. Anxieties in turn cause our nervous tensions, which we then convert into psychosomatic problems. These irrational assumptions are as follows:

1. A manager (we could substitute for the word *manager* the word *executive* or *person*) must be approved or liked by everyone for everything he does. What others think of him is most important; other people's feelings about him are more important than his own feelings about himself.

2. A manager should be thoroughly competent, adequate, talented, and intelligent in all possible respects. His main goal and purpose in life and work is achievement or success in *everything*. Incompetence in anything whatsoever is an indication that he is inadequate or valueless.

3. Because a certain thing once strongly affected a manager's life, it should indefinitely affect it. Because a manager once had a problem or made a mistake, it will continue to affect him throughout the remainder of his life.

4. If things are not the way the manager would like them to be, it is a catastrophe. Things should be better than they are. Other people should make life easier for managers and help them with their problems. No manager should have to put off present pleasures for future gains.

5. Most unhappiness is externally caused or created by other people and events. A manager has virtually no control over his emotions and cannot help feeling bad when things don't go his way.

6. If a manager's work is dangerous or possibly injurious, he

should be seriously concerned about it. Worrying about a possible danger will help ward it off or decrease its effect.

7. A manager should blame himself severely for all his mistakes and wrongdoings. Punishing himself for errors will help prevent future mistakes.

8. A manager should blame his subordinates for all their mistakes and wrongdoings. He should spend considerable time and energy trying to "straighten out" his people. Roundly criticizing and sharply pointing out the error of their ways are the best methods to help his subordinates.

9. If a manager wants something done right, he should do it himself. He should never trust his subordinates to do anything important. It doesn't matter that he is seriously overworked or that he really doesn't have time to carry out his principal responsibilities. If he does it himself, the job will be done his way, which is, after all, the best way.

10. A manager should always say what he thinks his superior wants to hear. He should never express his true emotions but should always suppress or deny his real feelings. Even though his ideas may be better than his superior's, he should never confront the boss, who wouldn't be in authority over him if he weren't older, wiser, and more experienced.

The unrealistic, irrational ideas causing a manager's anxiety are generally, at least in part, unconscious rather than conscious. Most managers often know consciously that it is naive and unrealistic to expect everyone to like them, to hope to do everything perfectly all the time, to be unable to stand any kind of frustration, or to worry about threatening possibilities. But unconsciously they firmly and deeply believe these assumptions, and again unconsciously they keep telling themselves over and over again that they should be liked, that they must do everything perfectly, that they should never be frustrated, that they should worry about possible mistakes and accidents. Their conscious views, therefore, are in direct conflict with their unconscious views; and, particularly since impossible desires are unattainable, they will become upset and anxious and will start building up nervous tensions, with the accompanying psychosomatic symptoms already discussed.

Evidence indicates that emotional factors have much to do with our general health. Furthermore, on certain occasions our emotions have everything to do with our health. What everyone must understand is the pressing need for adequate and effective emotional training as preparation for facing the problems they will encounter on their jobs in particular and in life in general. The need for a universal mental hygiene program is obvious. Human beings must come to understand their own natures and gain the knowledge necessary to deal effectively with their nervous tensions. Specifically, they must realize that most of their difficulties arise from overwhelming anxiety, and anxiety often arises out of ignorance of the facts. Intelligent education and training can remove much of the anxiety so many individuals carry about.

Remember that when a person employs one or more of the above-mentioned ten major irrational assumptions, one or two results will inevitably occur. One is that because he can't achieve his idealistic and impossible goals, he will become tense, depressed, guilty, hostile, or anxious. This, of course, will bring on psychosomatic problems. Or, two, he will set up psychological defenses to guard against consciously experiencing nervous tension or emotional pain. For example, he may rationalize, deny, project, lie, compensate, or take to alcohol or drugs.

Summing up, then, the main causes of people's problems are needless worry, anxiety, and unhappiness, which bring on behavior that is defensive, compulsive, or impulsive. The underlying reasons for this neurotic behavior are the irrational assumptions they have learned at some point in their lives—usually during their childhood—about life, work, and their interpersonal relationships.

References

Levi, Lenvart. *Stress*. New York: Liveright, 1967, p. 39.
Weiss, Edward. "Psychosomatic Aspects of Essential Hypertension." *Acta Psychotherapy* 2 1953, p. 28.

Selected Readings

Engel, George L. Studies of Ulcerative Colitis, 3. "The Nature of the Psychologic Processes," *American Journal of Medicine*, August 1955.
Fiske, C. E. "Personality and Emotional Factors in Chronic Disseminated

Neurodermatitis," Ph.D. dissertation, University of California at Los Angeles, 1956.

Friedman, Meyer, and Rosenman, Ray H. *Type A Behavior and Your Heart.* New York: Knopf, 1974.

Grinker, R. R. *Psychosomatic Research.* New York: Norton, 1953.

Miller, M. L. "Emotional Conflicts in Asthma," *Diseases of the Nervous System* 13 (1952).

Selye, H. "Adaptive Reaction to Stress," *Life, Stress and Bodily Diseases* 29 (1950):4.

Weiss, Edward, and English, Spurgeon O. *Psychosomatic Medicine: Its Principles and Applications.* Philadelphia: Saunders, 1943.

Wolf, Stewart. *The Stomach.* New York: Oxford University Press, 1965.

How to Help the Overweight Diet Successfully

I have a friend who has lost 240 pounds in the last twenty-four months. He has done this by losing twenty pounds one month and gaining it back the next. Consequently, he weighs the same today as he did two years ago because he keeps losing the same twenty pounds. As he and most dieters have discovered, it is easy enough to lose weight; keeping it off is not so easy.

Like every human behavior, eating, and especially overeating, is multidetermined. People eat not just because they have been without food for a while. They eat because their blood-sugar level has fallen, because brain mechanisms urge them to eat, because their stomachs are contracting, because their dinner time is approaching, or because they have just seen, smelled, or heard about something good to eat. Some people overeat because their parents thought fat babies were healthy and consequently overfed them when they were little. Other people overeat because of a morbid fear of starvation, particularly those who have gone without food for prolonged periods during childhood. Consciously, they are unaware of this phobia and therefore cannot adhere to dietary restrictions until they work through this problem. Other people overeat because of the subconscious secondary gains they receive, such as attention and feelings of importance acompanying vast bulk or size. In short, food is more than just something to eat. It takes on a variety of symbolic meanings, and, particularly for the obese person, it comes to represent some very complex social values. Obviously, then, any dieting program, to be successful, must take into account more than just calories and exercise. Psychological motives, personal mannerisms, and environmental factors must be considered as well if an obese person is to be successful in losing weight and maintaining the loss.

This multidetermination, then, is what makes unproductive the recommendation that everyone who eats too much should eat less and lose weight. That would be like prescribing aspirin for everyone who suffers from headaches. Some people consistently consume food and drink in excessive quantities to satisfy various emotional needs. Persistent overindulgence is an indication of some disturbance of physical and psychological equilibrium as certainly as a headache or a fever are symptoms of an organic illness in the body.

People who overindulge generally know it is harmful, but, beyond telling their doctor it relieves tension or that it is a family trait, they are unable to say much more. They rarely understand that they are eating or drinking excessively to compensate for emotional hunger or for their inability to discharge their feelings in more natural ways. For example, the obese person frequently takes on the role of a jovial, congenial person. This is often a reaction formation designed to cover up repressed feelings of hostility, often a major reason for their overindulgence.

It is a common observation that many persons who are not regularly given to overeating are inclined to do so during transient periods when the going is rough and living is difficult. For example, food and drink may temporarily compensate for the acute personal sense of insecurity occasioned by the death of a member of the family or the loss of a job.

Many patients request diets, and their doctors provide them on the assumption that anyone who wishes to follow a diet is able to do so. Such a notion is usually incorrect. Without examining these patients sufficiently to determine how satisfying or unsatisfying their lives may be, a doctor does not always serve the best interests of patients by prescribing a diet just because they request it. In one study, it was found that 93 percent of some 500 obese patients were aware of the relation between their eating patterns and their emotions. (Squires, 1958.)

The relative severity of a person's emotional conflict with respect to obesity can be described in one of the following categories.

1. Persons overeat as a substitute gratification in intolerable life situations.
2. Persons overeat as a response to nonspecific emotional tensions.
3. Persons overeat as a symptom of an underlying emotional illness, especialy depression or hysteria.
4. Persons overeat because of an addiction to food. (Nutrition Society, 1953.)

People who use the mechanism of the first two classes are relatively amenable to the measures used by physicians in their total care of a patient. The third class of people should be given a complete psychological evaluation to determine the cause and extent of their underlying emotional problems. The fourth class of people, who are addicted to food as some become addicted to drugs or alcohol, are sufficiently disturbed to require intensive and extensive counseling.

If external circumstances improve so that the obese individual receives satisfaction from other people, the need for food ingestion diminishes. This may help to explain why obesity is a psychological problem, in most cases, and also why remarkable "cures" are possible when circumstances permit a favorable realignment of the patient's activities. It also helps to explain the success of groups such as Weight Watchers, formed by obese persons and modeled after the order of Alcoholics Anonymous. These organizations offer much-needed companionship and realistic support to the obese person from other obese people who have an intimate appreciation of the powerful inner drives to eat.

Dr. E. Weiss cautions physicians about weight-reducing programs for patients in middie life. He states that

many of these people are hard-working men and women who unfortunately, for whatever reason, receive relatively little satisfaction from their families and jobs. These persons may be highly successful and important in their work but feel the need to overeat to give themselves pleasure. If one takes away food and drink from such a delicately balanced person, one has the obligation to put something constructive in its place. Due to the publicity about lung cancer, many patients have stopped smoking. For some this has resulted in considerable weight gains up to forty pounds. Now they dread the consequence of added weight. This is an example of the equivalence between one set of activities and another. (Weiss, 1953.)

Overeating and its opposite, the inability to eat, or anorexia, are two facets of a single process. The loss of desire to eat and the accompanying loss of weight likewise occurs in patients who suffer from depression and/or hysteria.

When some people eat less, they become unreasonable, irritable, quarrelsome, and sensitive. Other people become depressed, lose interest in work and social relations, develop insomnia, and think about suicide. The self-management of this problem is not simple. Those who succeed in giving up excessive eating often replace it with another overindulgence, such as drugs, which are even more harmful.

Business and social pressures contribute to the problems of overindulgence. Luncheons and dinner meetings are part of the pattern of modern living. These meetings often contribute to the problem of obesity due to the pressure to conform in these situations. To abstain from food and drink when entertained at these functions may be interpreted as a rude or unfriendly gesture. The obese person has a tremendous need to conform in order to be liked.

As mentioned previously, the mismanagement of the earliest mouth satisfactions in infants by naive parents prepares the pattern for excessive eating and drinking when an emotional disturbance or a crisis develops during later living. Obesity in adolescent girls, for example, is often the symptom of persistent dissatisfactions in the girls' relationships with their mothers. It is useless to expect such problems to be corrected by dieting. Their obesity is more displeasing to the mothers than to themselves. Their inability to reduce is an outward manifestation of the continuing vengeful feelings they have toward their mothers as well as the emotional satisfaction they get from eating. Successful management of such patients has often been achieved through the persistent kindness and understanding of family doctors and other specialists in the field of mental health. Excessive eating has been replaced by the satisfactions derived through the positive relationship developed between the patient and her doctor.

Overindulgence develops insiduously and without awareness of the dangers. It is significant that these excesses often occur at a time in life when human responsibility is at its height. At this period, most people are less active and more sedentary. Fatigue from work is more likely because work has assumed greater psychological importance. Men think of promotions with more responsibility, and women think of the increased responsibility of supervising the home and family. Extra food and drink relieve tensions and give one a false sense of emotional security.

In the light of our present knowledge of the emotional/psychological aspects of overindulgence, self-management may prove dangerous. The more intelligent course is to advise the patient to seek the services of her family doctor. Patient and doctor need to work in complete honesty with each other. They must be prepared for failure and disappointment and must become aware that weight management is generally slow and tedious but that it is possible, especially when the psychological problems responsible for overeating are worked through.

Above all, everyone should realize that today's diet fads, which promise quick and easy results, are developed for the naive among us. They simply do not work for long and serve primarily to make money for those who design and market them to a gullible public.

References

Nutrition Society. "The Psychology of Eating." *Lancet* 1 (1953):326-27.

Squires, A. H. "Emotions and the Diet." *Canadian Hospital* 1958, p. 70.

Weiss, E. "Psychosomatic Aspects of Dieting." *Journal of Clinical Nutrition* 1 (1953):140-48.

Selected Readings

Berlin, I., Boatman, M., and Sheima, S. "Adolescent Alteration of Anorexia and Obesity." *American Journal of Orthopsychiatry.* 21 (1951).

Grade, W. J., and Wolff, H. G. "The Night-eating Syndrome; A Pattern of Food Intake among Certain Obese Patients." *American Journal of Medicine* 19 (1955).

Kaplan, H. I., and Kaplan, H. S. "The Psychosomatic Concept of Obesity." *Journal of Nervous Mental Disorders* 125 (1957).

Lopez, I. J. "Obesity and Leanness As Ways of Life." *Review of Iber. Endocrinology* 3 (1956).

Randolph, T. H. "The Descriptive Features of Food Addiction: Addictive Eating and Drinking." *Quarterly Journal of Alcohol* 17 (1956).

Stunkard, A. J. "Untoward Reactions to Weight Reduction among Certain Obese Persons." *Ann. New York Acad. Sc.* 63 (1955).

Solez, C. "Overeating and Vascular Degeneration: Excesses Causing Insufficiencies." *Journal of American Geriatric Society* 6 (1958).

How to Help the Hypochondriac

A teenager I know is a chronic handwasher. He is so afraid of germs that whenever he touches anything "contaminated," he runs to the nearest sink and scrubs with soap and water. This youngster rarely gets sick—a fact that he attributes to his cautious nature—but his hands are always chapped and swollen and are a constant source of embarrassment to him. Lately he has withdrawn from his friends for fear of having to shake hands with them.

A relative of mine has a curious habit. He takes his temperature every morning when he gets up. He has no particular case history of disease and no other apparent reason for this routine, but he would no more think of leaving the house or even eating breakfast without performing this little ritual than most of us would think of skipping our morning showers.

A private nurse of my acquaintance always "catches" the disease of the patient she is taking care of. For fifteen years she has never failed to have, or think she has, the symptoms of her current patient's malady. In reality the very few illnesses she has experienced in this period have not coincided even remotely with her patients', but she continues to suffer from this peculiar contagion of the mind.

One of our neighborhood mothers, who has five children, the youngest now in his teens, lives in almost daily dread of polio. She and all her children have had their shots, and no case of the disease has been reported in our community for the last ten years; but in spite of this reassuring evidence, her fear has not diminished.

All four of these people are hypochondriacs suffering from a psychological disorder known as hypochondriasis, and, while their cases are more extreme than many, their malady is one that almost all of us can recognize from past personal experiences.

Hypochondriasis, the conviction that we are sick when we're not, or might get sick at any moment, attacks almost everyone at some time or another. Its symptoms are all too familiar—the mysterious racing heartbeat that convinces us a heart attack is imminent, the persistent cough that suddenly seems a sure sign of throat cancer, the sensation of dizziness that must mean a brain tumor. Perhaps it is a slight rash, a small lesion, a bump, a mole, an unaccounted-for black-and-blue spot, or something even less tangible—merely a vague sensation or a strange feeling that sets our mental mechanisms in motion.

What causes these fears? Mental health workers seem to agree that they have little or nothing to do with the state of our health and are not even basically related to a real concern for our health. Fundamentally they are not, as many imagine, a bid for attention. Hypochondriasis, instead, is an expression of guilt, not for something we've done, but for something we've felt. In imagining illness, we are punishing ourselves for what we consider our arrogant and extravagant fantasies, ambitions, and expectations.

This, of course, is a very complex psychological concept requiring a great deal of knowledge and experience in human psychology to understand fully. But even if your counselee doesn't completely understand the causes of her painful fears, there are things you can do to allay them. You can help her learn to distinguish, at least most of the time, between real and imaginary illness. This is actually simpler than it sounds because, like a real disease, hypochondriasis has its syndrome, or typical pattern of symptoms. Whatever the particular disease she thinks she has, the following clues usually indicate that it exists only in her mind.

1. *She feels worse when she's alone.* For some reason she tends to forget her fears in the company of others. The hypochondriac thrives on solitude, and her distress may disappear the minute other people are present.
2. *She puts off consulting a doctor.* Probably she tells herself she is

reluctant because she is afraid to hear his diagnosis. In reality, somewhere below her conscious level she knows she is not really sick and is afraid of his irritation or ridicule. When we are truly sick, our natural impulse is to get professional help as soon as possible.

3. *She has trouble putting her symptoms into words.* What she is feeling is not exactly a pain, not quite nausea, not really faintness, it's—well, more just a feeling that something is not right.

4. *The disease she fears she has is one she has thought she had before.* For reasons buried deep in her own subconscious, she fears one disease more than others. So, regardless of its likelihood, she returns to this particular malady whenever she feels—also subconsciously—that she deserves punishment. (Mead, 1965.)

Another helpful technique is the counselee's talking to someone about her fears. Obviously, a doctor is the person best qualified to advise her, and if any of her symptoms are of a tangible nature, by all means have her consult a professional. However, a sensible lay person can often help her break the unpleasant spell with nothing more than a little bit of sympathetic interest and some simple logic. It doesn't take a physician to say, "I know what you're going through because we all feel that way sometimes. But just look at yourself objectively, the way I see you. Your color is good, you have no sharp pains and no fever, and you are not bleeding or fainting. I honestly don't believe anything could be seriously wrong. Why not wait until tomorrow and see if you don't feel better?"

Just bringing these nameless monsters into the light of day makes them seem less terrifying. And the logic of another person's objective appraisal makes your counselee see things more realistically. If someone close to you is a hypochondriac, you can be helpful to them if you take the time to tell them why you believe they're not seriously ill. A few specific reasons can be infinitely more reassuring than an impatient, unconcerned statement that the person "looks like a million."

Hypochondriasis is no respecter of persons. It occurs among children and adults, men and women. It is by no means a mark of ignorance, since doctors and nurses are often among its recurrent victims, and it may be one of the reasons they chose medicine as a career in the first place. The exact nature of the hypochondriasis one is most likely to have is determined in part by the experiences of his family and friends, and, to some extent, on medical progress. When medicine produces an effective cure for a formerly highly dangerous, often fatal disease, that disease slowly recedes as a focus of fear. But such medical advances do not cure the hypochondriac; they merely transfer his fear to another disease.

Hypochondriasis is also transferable in another sense. It is possible for a hypochondriac to concentrate his fears not on his own health but on the well-being of another person. A wife may not imagine herself ill, but she might be constantly convinced that her husband is suffering from a fatal disease. A mother's fears of imagined illness may center in her child. And even the parent who repeatedly lies awake imagining automobile accidents until a teenaged son or daughter gets home at night could be called a hypochondriac.

Hypochondriasis has its positive side. It reminds us to avoid dangerous excesses and to take normal, sensible precautions about our health. For those who feel that pride can become excessive, it is an effective check on any such tendencies. Taking the brighter view, the false conviction of illness indicates that we have both imagination and ambition, two very vital ingredients to accomplishment. But being a hypochondriac is a negative way of expressing those qualities and a deterrent to realizing our full potential. So it's a wise precaution to encourage the hypochondriac to keep the antidote *logic* (his own or someone else's) at hand, to be administered quickly when he feels an attack of hypochondriasis coming on.

Just remember, if your counselee's mind is capable of convincing him that he is sick, it is also capable of convincing him that he is well.

Reference

Mead, B. T. "Management of Hypochondriacal Patients." *Journal of American Medical Association*, 1(1965):33N40.

Selected Readings

Busse, E. "The Treatment of the Chronic Complainer." *Med. Rec. Ann.* 50 (1956).

Chrzanowski, G. "Neurasthenia and Hypochondriasis." In *Comprehensive Textbook of Psychiatry*. Baltimore: Williams and Wilkins, 1967.

Dorfman, W. "Hypochondriasis as a Defense against Depression." *Psychosomatics* 9 (1968).

Greenberg, H. F. "Hypochondriasis." *Medical Journal*, 1 August 1960.

Kanner, L. "Hypochondriasis." In *Child Psychiatry*. Springfield: Charles Thomas, 1972.

Katzenelbozen, S. "Hypochondriacal Complaints with Specific Reference to Personality and Environment." *American Journal of Psychiatry* 98 (1941).

Kenyon, F. E. "Hypochondriasis: A Survey of Some Historical, Clinical, and Social Aspects." *Int. Journal of Psychiatry* 2 (1966).

Kreitman, N., Sainsbury, P., and Pierce, K. et al. "Hypochondriasis and Depression in Out-Patients at a General Hospital." *Br. Jr. Psychiatry* 3 (1965).

Laughlin, H. F. "Overconcern with Health—Somatic and Psychologic Preoccupation: Hypochondriasis." *Med. Ann. D.C.* 23 (1954).

Wahl, C. W. "Unconscious Factors in the Psychodynamics of the Hypochondriacal Patient." *Psychosomatics* 4 (1963).

Wahl, C. W. "Psychodynamics of the Hypochondriacal Patient." In *New Dimensions in Psychosomatic Medicine*. Boston: Little, Brown, 1964.

How to Help People Choose Mates

Not enough mention is made to people of the psychological danger signals they should be aware of in selecting mates. Scientific research has found that the following personality traits and characteristics either make or break a marriage. All young people (and older ones, too) contemplating this most important step in their lives should recognize these "red lights" and "amber lights" as if they were going in to take a test for a driver's license.

Young adults should beware of signs of jealousy in their prospective mates. At first jealousy may flatter the ego, but it will soon flatten life. A jealous mate simply cannot be lived with happily, and marriage takes giving on the part of each partner. Jealousy appears as a significant factor in at least one-half of all divorces. It arises out of many personality traits, all of which are undesirable. The jealous man is the frustrated, insecure, and uncertain individual. The jealous woman feels that people are not to be trusted (usually because she doesn't trust herself) and that life is threatening, dangerous, and unhappy. Attitudes like these are devastating to the close interpersonal relations in marriage.

If your counselee's "steady" is constantly alert for signs that his affection is waning or gives him the impression that she doesn't trust him, suggest to him that he give serious thought to breaking up the romance. Jealousy is not, as is commonly supposed, motivated by a profound love for another person; it is rather a form of self-love. The jealous person possesses strong narcissistic feelings. She is much more concerned with her own security, happiness, and welfare than the security, happiness, and welfare of the individual she professes to love.

Suggest to a counselee that she should shy away also from that person who has decided to dedicate his life toward making changes in her. Psychologists have learned that personality changes must occur before the marriage if, in general, they are to take place at all. Once the bonds are knit, people tend to remain what they are. Consequently, if one member of the wedded team assumes the task of "changing" the other, "flags" pop up all over the place. Marriage is mutual living in its finest guise, and mutuality suffers when the self-appointed straightener-outer enters the picture. If your counselee finds flaws she can't stand in her sweetheart, warn her to iron them out before the ceremony; she will reap only headaches if she waits until afterwards. Before she marries, by all means have her look beneath the glamour. Suggest that she know her prospective mate as he really is, not as she would like him to be, and accept or reject him on that basis. Warn her not to permit the living-togetherness of marriage to reveal her mate's true self to her for the first time. Encourage her to know herself and her future spouse as well. No marriage can survive a superior-inferior relationship, or any kind of an "I do, but you don't!" attitude. In marriage as in no other human relationship there must be equality. Souls lost before the wedding are seldom saved afterwards.

Suggest that she be cautious also if her beloved has a tendency to alibi or excuse bad behavior. The little white lies can lead to big black lies, and from there to serious misunderstandings. Anyone who is not strong enough to take responsibility for his misbehavior will be a slim reed to lean upon in times of stress. A good rule of thumb is that when the alibi is habitual, the emotions are immature. Small children characteristically blame other people or things for their failures, but an adult should have outgrown this. A person is foolish to handicap herself with an emotional infant for a spouse. Remember, excuses are attempts to evade responsibility, and a falsehood, white or black, remains a lie.

Suggest that a counselee be wary if his loved one tends to avoid responsibility through psychological escape mechanisms. Signs of this trait are sleepiness in times of stress, withdrawal when feelings are hurt, and retreat of any kind when things go wrong. Common retreats are sulking; escape into movies, TV, books, or music; and taking drugs or alcohol. If a boyfriend or a girlfriend needs a pill or a drink in order to cope with life's problems, it would be better for the intended partner to find someone more emotionally mature. Little habits like these grow greater as marriage ages. The person who tries to escape from reality, in whatever manner, will be extremely difficult to live with. If your counselee chooses to marry such a person, he can be sure that all problems will wait for him to solve. His spouse will be asleep, reading, at the movies, daydreaming, spaced out on drugs, or drunk at just the time he will have greatest need for her. If you marry the escapist, plan on carrying a double load.

And there is the problem of in-laws. Like it or not, when a couple marry, they also unite with their spouse's family. In a very real sense, they join a fraternity of relatives. If your counselee plans to live within easy traveling distance of them, have her look the members over carefully. Most mothers-in-law are great, but some can create great problems. The mother who has smothered her own child will also try to smother her daughter-in-law.

Your counselee should be particularly alert for the male who has made a game of conquest out of love. She can be reasonably sure that when the novelty of marriage wears off, this character will begin to look about for unconquered territory. She should not expect the habitual flirt to be considerate of her. The behavior itself tells her that his only interest is self-interest. The chances are good that she will shortly play background music for the dalliance his shaky personality needs. Through his conquests he proves to himself that he is a real person after all. If he adds up to be a true "wolf," encourage her to let him run. No trap, however tender, will hold him for long. Summing up, those persons who cannot really love another are those who (Landis, Landis, 1958):

1. Are emotionally immature and hence not capable of love as a sharing proposition.
2. Have an inordinate attachment to a parent and therefore, while they can transfer this attachment to an agemate, cannot really love their spouse except as a kind of parent substitute.

3. Are so egocentric and/or narcissistic that they cannot love another except as a sort of mirror that reflects their own infinite desirability.
4. Feel a predatory attitude toward the opposite sex. To these a spouse can never be a genuine love object but at best becomes a means for self-gratification.
5. Have a fearful attitude toward sex; although they can simulate love physically, they cannot really love emotionally.
6. Possess a basic insecurity and need for attention. For these love is a compulsive, driven, neurotic search for security.
7. Use love as a means of escaping from an undesirable home or social situation.
8. Are homosexual, since love for one's own sex is incompatible with heterosexual love.
9. Feel so inadequate or inferior that they cannot imagine anyone finding them to be desirable. Their basic attitude is, "I wouldn't marry anyone who would have me as a mate." In a nutshell, people who cannot accept themselves will be unable to love.

The kinds of personality problems mentioned above are classified by psychologists as neurotic behavior. A neurosis is, simply stated, a disturbance in human relations. Marriage is the epitome of human relations; it is two people living together. Therefore, evidence of neurotic symptoms in a prospective mate should make the partner wary. If your counselee detects indications of strong insecurity or any of the other characteristics of emotional maladjustment, tell him or her to keep looking, or get some professional help. If disturbances basic to neurotic trends are present in either partner, the odds are that the responsibilities of marriage will increase their role in the life of that person. Marriage has never cured a neurosis, but it has brought many into full bloom. Therefore, to hope that "things will be different after we're married" is to live in ignorance. Things will most certainly be different, but not quite in the way your counselee hopes. Young people, and others seeking mates, must learn the standards of good adjustment. During courtship they should measure themselves and their prospective mates against these standards. Any extensive deviation from the norm is grounds for concern and caution.

The following are some of the characteristics of the emotionally mature individual (a card issued by the National Association of Mental Health):

They feel comfortable about themselves.
1. They are not bowled over by their own emotions—by their fears, anger, love, jealousy, guilt, or worries.
2. They can take life's disappointments in their stride.
3. They have a tolerant, easy-going attitude toward themselves as well as others; they can laugh at themselves.
4. They neither underestimate nor overestimate their abilities.
5. They can accept their own shortcomings.
6. They have self-respect.
7. They feel able to deal with most situations that come their way.
8. They get satisfaction from simple, everyday pleasures.

They feel right about other people.
1. They are able to give love and to consider the interests of others.
2. They have personal relationships that are satisfying and lasting.
3. They expect to like and trust others, and they take it for granted that others will like and trust them.
4. They respect the many differences they find in people.
5. They do not push people around, nor do they allow themselves to be pushed around.
6. They can feel they are part of a group.
7. They feel a sense of responsibility to their neighbors and fellowmen.

They are able to meet the demands of life.
1. They do something about their problems as they arise.
2. They accept their responsibilities.
3. They shape their environment whenever possible; they adjust to it when necessary.
4. They plan ahead but do not fear the future.
5. They welcome new experiences and new ideas.
6. They make use of their natural capacities.
7. They set realistic goals for themselves.
8. They are able to think for themselves and make their own decisions.

9. They put their best effort into what they do, and they get satisfaction out of doing it.

Most divorces occur in the first years of marriage. The prime reason for this is that wedlock is so intimate that flaws in human makeup are soon revealed. Furthermore, the decision to take divorce action is commonly made within the first few months after the wedding, although it may be much later that the divorce is worked out legally. The best way to prevent divorce is to make sure that you make a good choice in the first place. While we humans will always err, you can reduce the probability of error in marriage by a careful checkout before you take this most important step.

In responding to the question: "Is she really for me?" a counselee should honestly answer the following ten questions (Dunlap, 1946). If he can answer all ten of them with an objective "yes," the odds for a happy marriage are in his favor.* However, if he has to say "no" to but one of them, he should be cautious indeed.

1. Am I happier with her than I am with any other person?
2. When I am not with her, am I persistently wishing for her company, or does some other person put her out of my mind?
3. Would I be not only willing but happy to spend my life with her, centering my other interests about her?
4. Would I gladly give up all my interests and activities that do not conform with my devoting my life interest to her?
5. Is she the one person whom I would choose, above all others, to be the mother of my children?
6. Do I love her with her faults of face, figure, disposition, or education (for she has faults, and I know it); do I even love those faults or defects themselves as being essential parts of her?
7. Is she apparently disposed to make for me sacrifices as great as those I am willing to make for her?
8. Is she disposed to adapt herself to me to a reasonable extent in interests, temperamental matters, and other ways, or does

---

*The masculine and feminine pronouns may be interchanged in this questionnaire.

72

she expect me to do all the adapting?
9. Is there a community of interests, culture, and education adequate to a joint life with her?
10. Do I like her family well enough to be able to tolerate them and get along with them, or, if not, is it fairly certain that I won't have to associate with them?

Observe that the first three questions bear upon those aspects of courtship that are typical of teenage, romantic love. Most adolescents in the throes of their first romance would answer "yes" enthusiastically to the first three items. However, the remaining seven questions should give anyone reason to pause and think. Questions 4 through 10 are designed to seriously predict an individual's probable success in marriage. If your counselee was able to give an honest, unqualified "yes" to each question, the one of his choice is probably right for him.

Now, if he passed the first test, the following questionnaire (Terman, 1938) includes ten background factors that he should answer to predict his marital success:
1. Were your parents happily married?
2. Did you have a happy childhood?
3. Was there an absence of serious conflict with your mother and father?
4. Was there firm, but not harsh, discipline in your home?
5. Do you have a strong affectional attachment to both of your parents?
6. Was there mild and infrequent childhood punishment?
7. Were your premarital attitudes free from disgust, fear, or aversion?
8. Was there parental frankness and objectivity in your sexual education?
9. Was your engagement long enough to permit a thorough acquaintance with your prospective mate?
10. Was there similarity in your religious, social, educational, and economic backgrounds?

You will notice that at least eight of the above background factors predictive of marital happiness are determined by early life experiences in the home. Thus we see the deep importance that the homelife of a child carries for its later good emotional adjustment as an adult.

In addition to the ten personal-preference questions and the ten background questions, your counselee can further estimate his probable success in marriage with the following twenty-question personality test (Adams and Packard, 1946):

1. Can you be depended upon to finish a job you have begun?
2. Were you happy as a child?
3. Are you free from morbid thoughts and fears about sex?
4. Can you decide things for yourself easily and without worry?
5. Are you objective with yourself and others?
6. Are you free from acute sensitivity so that you are not easily hurt?
7. Do you like people?
8. Do you get along readily with people?
9. Can you accept suggestions from others without feeling imposed upon?
10. Can you adapt yourself easily to new situations and events?
11. Do you stop and think rather than decide in terms of your feelings?
12. Do you try to see things from the other person's point of view?
13. Are you usually calm and relaxed?
14. Are you concerned about what other people think of you?
15. Do you believe in the standards, ideals, and morals of good social conduct?
16. Are you interested in many things?
17. Are you generally happy and pleasant?
18. Are you considerate of the feelings of others?
19. Do you feel content with life?
20. Is your emotional life smooth and even rather than continuously up and down?

If prospective mates can answer all forty items with an honest "yes," both are excellent marital risks. Wherever they had to say "no" to a question, have them sit down and ask themselves some more questions. Try to find out why they had to say "no," then look into the possibility of their so changing themselves that the answer will become "yes." Discover what they must do in order to make the necessary changes; then decide whether or not they are willing to pay the price to do so.

Unfortunately, they will be unable to change some of the "no" answers in their background factors; they must simply accept them and strive not to let them influence their actions unduly. They cannot change the past. They can learn from it, however, and make sure they don't make the same mistakes with their children that their parents made with them.

Now, supposing most of their answers on the forty questions were "no." They should realize that they are very poor marital risks. Why? Because they are not grown up emotionally; their thinking is mostly wishing, and, if they can't change, they will no doubt be a pain in the neck to each other.

According to the *Salt Lake Tribune*, March 9, 1976, between the years 1965 and 1975 the divorce rate in the state of Utah increased 76 percent; the national divorce rate increased 92 percent (the Utah Bureau of Health Statistics). Studies have identified one of the main reasons for the high divorce rate: the large number of teenage marriages. Nationally, approximately one-third of all women who marry are under 20 years of age. In Utah during the year 1972, 43 percent of all women marrying were teenagers. It is highly doubtful that these young brides or their young husbands were mentally, emotionally, or spiritually prepared for the tremendous responsibilities of marriage and therefore contributed heavily to Utah's rapidly increasing divorce rate.

Parents, schools, and churches must strive diligently to teach people how to become mature men and women so that they can make proper marital choices. If they do not succeed in helping people make this most important decision, they too, must assume at least part of the blame for marital failures.

References

Adams, C., and V. Packard. *How to Pick a Mate.* New York: Dutton, 1946, p. 58.

Dunlap, K. *Personal Adjustment.* New York: McGraw-Hill, 1946, p. 323.

Terman, L. M. *Psychological Factors in Marital Happiness.* New York: McGraw-Hill, 1938, p. 372.

Selected Readings

Duvall, E., and R. Hill. *When You Marry.* New York: Associated Press, 1945.

Landis, J. T., and M. Landis. *Building a Successful Marriage.* Englewood Cliffs, New Jersey: Prentice-Hall, 1958.

Strain, F. *Marriage Is for Two.* New York: Longmans, Green, 1955.

How to Help Couples Stay Happily Married

The time for a couple to seek counseling is before their conflicts reach the stage where they are seriously considering divorce. Counseling should be sought jointly. Whether the issue involves one or all five of the most common marital problems—communication, money, children, in-laws, or sex—the first step should be to find an impartial umpire to arbitrate the dispute. Married couples would be well advised not to go to relatives or friends with the details of their disagreements. This procedure does nothing but deepen fighting ranks on both sides without removing the cause of the feud.

Many couples fear going to a marriage counselor because they have heard that he frequently recommends divorce. The wife will come in and say, "My husband won't come. He's afraid you'll say our marriage is hopeless, and the only thing left to do is break up." Or both will warn me in advance, "We want to get one thing straight, Doctor; we don't want a divorce. We're not getting along right now, but we do want to stay married."

No one knows better than a marriage counselor that divorce is not the best answer to marital conflicts but that it generally brings many more problems in its wake. The divorce may remove one source of friction, but the causes of the problem still hold sway over the personalities of the man and woman. Very few cases of incompatibility are wholly one-sided—one partner altogether guilty and the other altogether innocent; the tyrant must be married to a martyr, or he can't get away with his tyrannical behavior.

The whole object of marriage counseling is to improve the relationship, not undermine it. Marriage counselors spare no effort to save a marriage in every possible case, especially when children are involved, because in any divorce the children always suffer the most. However, a counselor does not try to mislead a couple by offering false assurances. He cannot guarantee to save any marriage. Some marriages have developed such intense strains and stresses that they constitute a torture chamber for the participants rather than the haven that poets speak about. Though it may appear obvious that a particular marriage will never last, a counselor does not say point-blank, "I'd give up the struggle and get an immediate divorce." He acts in the capacity of a guide, not a dictator, to the troubled pair. He points out the source of the difficulty, then tries to educate them to correct it. Even after counseling, a husband may be unwilling to stop drinking, or a wife may be unable to give up her dependency on drugs. Unfortunately, there are times when a couple will decide the cure is worse than the disease and will choose to keep their problems. If that is the case, the counselor will never strong-arm them into a different decision but will give whatever assistance is indicated.

Since there is so much ballyhoo about the business of seeing a marriage counselor, I would like you to accompany an unhappily married pair to my office to see what really goes on there. In the first interview the couple come together if that is at all possible. The wife usually tells her story first, without interruption. Then the husband tells his, without interruption. I warn both in advance that I am the judge in this courtroom scene and will not tolerate any shouting, abuse, or cutting in by one on the other partner's statements. In outlining their problems to me, both discover that it is possible to talk about their grievances without exploding and listen to the other's point of view with adult self-control.

I have found it wise not to jump to conclusions based on what I hear in the first interview. In every marital conflict there are always three versions to the story—hers, his, and the real story, which lies somewhere in between. She may say, "He's not a good provider." He may respond with, "She doesn't know how to budget." At first it would appear that the contended issue is the family finances, but the deeper, more important conflict may involve the emotional insecurity of one or both of the partners.

After the joint interview, I administer personality tests to both the husband and the wife to help determine the real cause of their underlying emotional problems, after which they come in both separately and jointly for as many sessions as are needed to help them gain insight into their maladjustments. It may take only a few interviews to clear the air; or it may be that one partner is suffering from a deep-seated personality disorder such as paranoia, causing a persistent, unrealistic feeling of jealousy. Or one of the mates may be experiencing a manic-depressive reaction that consists of emotional highs and lows. Both of these emotional problems are serious indeed and usually require long-term counseling.

If children are involved in their parents' disagreements, it is important that they sit in on some of the discussions also, in what is currently called *conjoint family therapy*. Adolescents, especially, often have great insight into their parents' problems and can make valuable contributions toward keeping the home and family together. (Satir, 1964.)

During the treatment procedure I request that the husband, wife, and children, if indicated, let off steam toward each other in my presence. Again, I remind them that I am the judge for this period in their marriage. I hear all the evidence, act as the arbitrator in this noisy courtroom dispute, and insist that order be maintained. While this process continues from week to week, all the sources of friction are probed and worked through. The husband and wife are then helped to develop certain basic problem-solving skills and attitudes which, hopefully, will serve as future-guides for increased harmony in their marriage.

Every married couple should know that the main cause of marital disharmony is *selfishness*. When we get to the core of human behavior, selfishness and pride are two of our most powerful emotions. Selfishly we protect our bodily comfort at another's expense, and selfishly we protect our ego at someone else's expense. In marriage these protective mechanisms often balloon out of proportion when our comfort or ego is threatened. A wife who runs over her budget to buy a few little fond and foolish things will find her husband furious over the small threat to his security. He will crack down on her in the hope of preventing such inroads into his income in the future. He may well succeed in his aim—only to have an unhappy wife who returns his grudging treatment with poor meals, a dirty house, or disappointing nights.

We all have a tendency to want, rather than to give. We want security, kindness, love, attention, respect, success. We want as much as we can get in material things—a better home, a better car, a better boat, and better clothes. Unfortunately, these "things" have become the yardstick for success in our culture in these modern times. In marriage our wants begin to conflict with our actual needs and, especially, the needs of our loved ones. The generous concern, the courtesy, the politeness, the mutual sharing of courtship days break down. We become more possessive, more demanding toward our partner. A whole evening can be wrecked over which TV show to watch or who should pay the paper boy. The winner feels triumphant; the loser is resentful. It becomes a matter of pride not to give in on that issue the next time. In practically every marriage, to some extent, a constant power struggle takes place. Couples seem forever engaged in playing the game of one-upmanship. This, of course, can be a devastating game depending upon the maturity of the married couple. I have found in my practice that generally the husband is more demanding and more selfish than the wife. He wants sexual relations when he prefers them without much regard for his spouse's feelings. In addition, he wants a wife who is a good manager, maid, cook, companion, and mother. There are more reasons for this type of male chauvinism than selfishness alone. Sometimes it occurs in the name of patriarchal authority. In any case, the male of the species seems to demand more than the female.

A woman, once married, usually feels more relaxed, more secure. She has a man to earn the living, provide the home, and protect the family. A man, once married, is only at the beginning of new frustrations. Many firsts come as unexpected and painful experiences to him. His freedom is curtailed. Bills arrive every month, the size of which he has never before seen. He begins to weigh the responsibilities, and they sometimes loom so large he can't see around them to the other aspects of his marriage. He then begins to analyze his marriage, like a shrewd businessman, in terms of a return on his investment. He might say, "How much am I really getting out of this marriage?" or "Did I get the best kind of bargain in my wife?" or "Could I have done better?" Interestingly, this kind of man rarely stops to ask himself if he is a jewel as a husband and father. When the husband isn't as successful as he had hoped to be, he often becomes more unreasonable and demanding. If he doesn't earn well or doesn't gain enough prestige from his coworkers, he will often displace his resentment and hostilities on his unsuspecting wife. He can project his anger toward her because she is a safe target to blame for his failures.

In counseling couples I have told many a complaining husband, "True, you are providing a home and paying the bills, but in exchange for sustenance your wife has to put up with coldness, indifference, and abuse. You break out in temper tantrums when things don't go your way. You leave all the child care to her and do not take the time to be a good father to the children you brought into the world. Golf, television, fishing, and hunting seem more important to you than your family. Your wife is very close to the end of her rope, and you could easily be the cause of her having an emotional breakdown." Every man needs to take a periodic inventory of himself as a husband and father. He needs to estimate his own selfishness and change his negative attitudes and poor habit patterns toward his wife and children before it is too late.

Sometimes it is the wife who needs to analyze her failings. She may be too domineering, indifferent, or neglectful toward her husband as she becomes absorbed in the home and children. She may belittle him in his role of family provider or take him for granted, making him feel that he is not very important. She may be insensitive to the kind of pressure her husband feels on the job, neglecting to give him the emotional support and encouragement he needs to face his work problems. She may be too tired at night or too wound up over the household chores to take time to pretty herself or give him warm response in love.

We all need to estimate, on a regular basis, our own selfishness, in order to test it consciously and keep it in check. I am continuously surprised and gratified with the results obtained by married couples who practice this one simple precept, unselfishness, to regain their harmony and the mutual regard that attracted them during their courting days.

Compromise is another essential in the art of staying married. Every marriage from time to time will tangle with painful realities such as sickness, children's problems, debts, and various other responsibilities. Invariably, husbands and wives have different points of view: clashes over child rearing, or how to spend the money, or where to take the next vacation, or any of a host of other issues. Compromise and mutual consideration are vital to making correct decisions. Neither member of the married pair has the right to demand the final say in all things. I have seen marriages fail because all the compromising was done by only one of the partners. When only one person compromises and the other doesn't, the one-sidedness of the marriage makes it list in rough times like a ship with a badly weighted cargo. One person cannot continue giving in, making all the compromises, smoothing over all the disagreeable situations indefinitely. Rebellion is inevitable, sooner or later, in one form or another. This is a matter of personality rather than education or lack of it. I have found that ordinarily well-mannered and intelligent men and women can become deadlocked in a competitive marriage or in a war of temperaments and wills simply because of their insecure personalities.

Criticism is considered one of the prerogatives of marriage. It is more apt to be a prerogative of divorce. The wife who establishes herself as her husband's severest critic is not his best friend. One's best friend is one's most tactful and diplomatic critic and one's strongest booster. The knock without the boost will not gain a husband's thanks. He may act on the criticism, but he will inwardly resent the way it was offered.

The same holds true for the overcritical husband. There is much said about the way wives criticize their husbands, but in my experience I have found husbands to be much more critical of and demeaning to their wives. Wives often become pecky about a husband's clothes or his failure to show more polish in his manners. It is a superficial type of criticism that is usually exasperating but is not contradictory to her basic sense of loyalty. A husband's criticism, when he is the ridiculing type, is likely to go much deeper. A man who becomes wealthy or successful can also become very cruelly critical of the woman he married before he had the money and the success. He often succeeds in undermining every vestige of her faith in herself as an individual. This sort of husband literally takes his wife apart. He ridicules the way she does her hair, the way she pronounces her words, the kind of conversation she makes or fails to make, the fact that she is not as glamorous or as cultured as he believes she should be. He, of course, does not give himself any such searching analysis. Despite the facts that his income has added three more zeros and his home, cars, and boat are impressive, he may be as gauche and as ungrammatical and blatant in his tastes as he was when he started on the lower rungs of the success ladder.

No marriage can be happy or can keep its faith intact when one partner must go on being a target for the other's digs and put-downs year in and year out. No one has the right to crush another's self-esteem. Adults, like children, learn best and improve most when suggestions and corrections are made in kindly tones rather than by shouting or sarcasm.

Often a wife hurts herself deeply by clinging to her own worst traits. Her husband's criticism makes her stubborn. She says, "I won't try to change until he treats me better." Wives should realize that they hurt no one but themselves when they deliberately let their appearance decline by acquiring twenty-five extra pounds from the solace of cake or candy. They are taking their frustrations out on themselves, not on their husbands. This merely gives him grounds for additional criticism.

When a wife tells me that she has lost all confidence in herself because of her overly critical husband, I tell her to dry her eyes; the crying will do no good. What she must do is not let the critical husband know that he is hurting her. She should then make whatever improvements she can in herself along the lines he has been harping on. But her motive must be self-improvement, not appeasement of his displeasure. A self-improved wife at the same time becomes more attractive in the eyes of her friends and neighbors. Praise and admiration of his wife from others is sometimes all that is needed to awaken a husband to a shamefaced realization of his own blindness to her good qualities.

There is another side to this question of criticism. Oversensitive people who can't take any criticism at all, even when constructively and kindly given, are likely to prove failures in marriage. For physically sensitive allergics, medicine has discovered desensitizers to combat the overreaction that sends them into paroxysms of sneezing at the touch of a feather or the sight of a strawberry. For oversensitive marital partners, no known saving medicine exists. These people have to learn to desensitize themselves to the slighting word and the thoughtless, belittling act of a spouse. In marriage, criticism must always be evaluated according to intent. If the comment is casual or heedless, mates must train themselves to let it slide off without doing damage. If the partner's criticism is consistent and is deliberately aimed and timed to hurt the worst, that is a different story. This calls for an overhaul. For the little, garden-variety wisecrack, married people need only training in keeping their feathers flat and not permitting their spouses to ruffle them too easily. It can become a lifelong game, however, for a husband or wife to rile up the partner just for the fun of it, if the reaction is interestingly explosive. Remember that overreaction is almost always a sign of insecurity in any situation involving a threat to what we feel is our best welfare.

Maintenance of a good sexual relationship is absolutely vital to an enduring marriage. Even in the most harmonious marriage, the sexual relationship cannot be put on a shelf while a husband devotes himself to his job or his hobby for several months. Neither can it be put aside while the wife devotes herself to a child's lingering illness. No words are more fatal to a marriage than, "We'll get together again after this trouble is all behind us."

The physical relationship in marriage needs to be good from week to week. When it lapses, a crack opens in the marriage. The wife begins to suspect that the husband's failure to approach her is not merely business fatigue but that his love for her is fading. The need for reassurance from the physical relationship is something that does not stop, no matter what else may happen. There may be domestic troubles, quarrels, illness, bills to pay, and work to be made up, but none of these things alters the need for continuing love. They only make it more necessary to the health and well-being of the husband and wife.

When I am visited by couples who have cooled off toward each other physically because of some problem, my first recommendation is that they resume sexual relations during counseling. They often balk at the idea and ask, "Wouldn't it be better if we wait until after we have settled our differences?" My answer is, "No! It can't wait." Putting off the demonstration of love in marriage keeps a barrier of pride and tension between them. One way of getting around that pride is for me to be the one to insist that they resume their relations while they try to solve their other problems.

I have found that if the trouble with the marriage is sex itself, the partners are very reluctant to try to resume love-making during treatment. Their argument is, "But, Doctor, sexual incompatibility is our problem. What good will it do to go back to it now?" My answer is that clumsy dancers do not learn to dance well by giving up dancing. They must practice, study, and learn all there is to know about acquiring grace and rhythm as these movements apply to dancing. Love-making is very similar. The partners may need re-education and instruction in better techniques which can be applied to their performance. In any case, they must not give up their sexual relations, or it will most surely ruin their marriage.

The way two individuals face possible disaster is often a deciding factor in preventing the disaster. A man and woman can stand on the edge of a precipice and talk without too much danger. If they engage in a shouting quarrel, the chances are the quarrel will end in a tussle and both will go over the edge. No battle or contest has ever been won by a hysterical combatant. In marriage, as in everything else, great satisfaction is derived from not running away from problems but meeting the challenge and overcoming the difficulties. Nothing else in life can equal this satisfaction.

Much of the unhappiness that arises in marriage can be avoided if husband and wife can adopt a philosophy of mutual consideration. Any good philosophy needs practical daily expression to keep it alive. Here are ten working suggestions for couples who want not only to stay married but to make their marriage an everlasting pleasure.

1. Limit criticism to a minimum. Keep praise at the maximum.

2. Adopt a courtroom technique for arguments. Make them discussions, not verbal battles.
3. Give conversation its due; make it enjoyable by cutting down on recitals of complaints, ailments, bills, and worries.
4. Put a stop to sulking, profanity, and name-calling before they become a habit.
5. Examine yourself for your own failings when you are tempted to brood over your partner's.
6. Kill the impulse to arouse suspicion and jealousy in your partner with reports of flirtatious encounters, or you will destroy your relationship.
7. Consult with each other on the family budget; come to an agreement on financial matters.
8. Don't forget to use the common courtesies with each other, such as "please," "thank you," and "you're welcome."
9. Remember each other's birthdays, anniversaries, holidays, and special events with cards, gifts, candy, and flowers.
10. Have fun, but have it together; marriage falls flat without shared good times to give it sparkle.

References

Satir, Virginia. *Conjoint Family Therapy*. Palo Alto, California: Science and Behavior Books, 1964, p. 163.

Selected Readings

Ackerman, Nathan W. *Treating the Troubled Family*. New York: Basic Books, 1966.

Horney, Karen. *Feminine Psychology*. New York: Norton, 1967.

Jackson, Donald. *Human Communication*. Palo Alto, California: Science and Behavior Books, 1968.

Klemer, Richard H. *Counseling in Marital and Sexual Problems*. Baltimore: Williams and Wilkins, 1965.

Rosenbaum, S., and Alger, I. *The Marriage Relationship*. New York: Basic Books, 1968.

Silverman, H. L., ed. *Marital Counseling*. Springfield, Illinois: Thomas, 1967.

How to Help Avoid a Broken Home

Most of my patients come from broken homes; this fact has always been of great concern to me. In counseling couples with marital problems, I always point out what the dissolution of their marriage will likely do to their children. Sometimes I am heard; more often, however, my warning falls on deaf ears.

Over the years, I have looked into the faces of countless disturbed youngsters and said, "You know, I could 'cure' you if I could just put you in a good home." I'm convinced that broken homes cause most of the emotional problems in the world today and that a city, a state, or a nation is truly only as strong as its homes.

A broken home is usually thought of as one where the parents have been divorced or where one of the parents is deceased. But to a slightly lesser degree it also includes homes where the parents are separated or where one, usually the father, is engaged in some activitiy that requires him to be away from home a great deal of the time. Wives of servicemen who are abroad or of salesmen who are on the road for extended trips or of businessmen who boast about working 16 hours a day often consider themselves "widows" and are rightfully concerned about the effect of the missing parent on their children. Homes in which both parents are physically present but where one or the other is psychologically unable to function as a parent or spouse also constitute part of the broken-home syndrome. Homes broken by divorce are, of course, the most serious because the emotional factors surrounding a divorce make it particularly difficult for the children to cope with the problems involved.

The greatest trauma seems to occur if the home is broken before a child reaches the age of eight (or the age of account-ability) or before the latency period begins. The personality iden-tification as well as the psychosexual development of a child are in great jeopardy if the home is fragmented before the child has been able to properly work through this early, crucial stage of his or her development.

The major cause of children's problems, however, is not the absence of one parent but the way the child is treated and the way the child perceives the parents' relationship with each other and with himself. Many children from broken homes are able to make a totally acceptable adjustment to society, though they usu-ally suffer to a greater or lesser degree in the process. It would be impossible, however, to obtain statistical data on their relative numbers as compared to those children who do not make a satisfactory adaptation following the breakup of their home.

The most outstanding phenomenon in children from broken homes is the presence of a profound depression. Some of the children are able to conceal their unhappiness, but the depres-sion remains and is likely to emerge in various other forms. Academic failure, running away from home, antisocial behavior, shoplifting, sleeping difficulties, inability to concentrate, appetite disturbances, drug and alcohol addiction, psychosomatic symp-toms, preoccupation with morbid thoughts, and suicidal rumina-tions are all symptoms of stress brought on by depression.

In a large private neuropsychiatric hospital where I recently worked, all the adolescents undergoing treatment for drug abuse came from broken homes. Some of the youngsters were quite bitter in their attitude toward their parents. Others accepted their fate stoically as something that had happened in the past, while failing to recognize how their parents' divorce had created the feelings of insecurity, inadequacy, and inferiority that led to ex-perimentation and gradual addiction to drugs.

Although depression is the most outstanding and universal characteristic in children from broken homes, one must bear in mind the two factors on which the depression is based—guilt and rejection. To illustrate, let me tell you about a young patient I worked with for many years. I first saw this boy at age six for a stuttering problem. Probing into the family dynamics, I discovered that his parents were having serious marital problems. They had been arguing and bickering for years, and the boy generally took the brunt of the displaced hostility they felt toward each other. The parents separated when the boy was eight and finally divorced when he was ten. When asked if he felt responsible for his parents' divorce, his answer was, "Of course it was my fault."

Before the separation he was required to be a model child. His father insisted that he appear for meals well scrubbed and extremely neat. If his personal appearance did not meet with the father's approval, the man would turn on the mother and angrily denounce her, saying, "It is your fault that this boy does not conform to my standards of conduct. You are a failure as a wife and mother and I will not put up with any more of this." After the separation and divorce, this youngster lived with his mother and would see his father only during a required once-a-year visit, a traumatic experience for him both in anticipation and in actuality. At age twelve his mother placed him in a military school—an act that he interpreted as total rejection by her. At the first opportunity he went AWOL from the school. He was soon found but refused to return to live with his mother; and as his father would not accept him, he was placed in a foster home.

In the ensuing four years he was transferred to six different foster homes, and his juvenile delinquency record was extensive. It included such charges as shoplifting, breaking and entering, theft, possession of stolen property, malicious mischief, truancy, and incorrigibility. This young man was now suffering from what psychologists refer to as "Nero's neurosis." Nero, who is said to have fiddled while Rome burned was reported to have said, "Tis better to go down in history as a no-good scoundrel than not to go down in history at all." Psychologically speaking, this statement means that any kind of attention, even negative attention, is better than no attention at all. In just four short years this young man had managed to attract the interest and attention of many important people, including policemen, judges, lawyers, psychologists, psychiatrists, social workers, and religious leaders. At one point he made the statement that he intended to go out and commit more crimes to see who else he could get interested in him. He did exactly that. At age nineteen he is dead, killed in a shootout with a policeman during an armed robbery. What a waste of a human life and what a tragedy! And it all began with the breakup of his home.

We who work in the field of counseling see many types of symptoms in children who are suffering from the tension and strain of a broken home. These include such psychosomatic illnesses as headaches, stomachaches, muscular aches and pains, nervous tics, rashes on the skin, and general fatigue. Emotional and behavioral disturbances are also frequently manifested. Truancy and running away from home are common occurrences, and delinquent behavior such as mugging, stealing, sexual acting-out, and drug and alcohol abuse are almost always cries for help. These various disturbed behaviors are usually motivated not only by the child's need for attention and for care and concern by the significant figures in his life, but also by his need for treatment to relieve the psychological and physical pain from which he is suffering. Counseling with children is difficult and not always successful. Often, however, it can help alter the picture and start youngsters on a healthier, more positive path. The time factor is of vital importance. If children are given help at the time of divorce or separation, their prognosis is significantly better. The longer the broken home continues without the children's receiving guidance and emotional support, the more difficult it is to work toward restoring the various components of their personalities.

One of the saddest situations is that of a child being used as a football to be kicked between the divorced mother and father. Visiting rights and the care of the child become means by which one parent can antagonize or punish the other. Such individuals are not only immature but are acting in a selfish manner to gratify their own needs and desire for revenge rather than trying to understand the child's need for stability and love at this critical period in his or her life. Effective intervention by some professional person or organization in this type of pathological situation can be of immense help to the victimized child.

The economic status of parents is not a factor of particular importance in these situations. Publicover (1965) found in his research that public-school children from poor homes displayed the same reactions and responses as children in private schools who came from affluent homes. What is far more important is the degree to which depression, guilt, fear of rejection, and anxiety over impending visits or remarriage have been aroused in the children by their insensitive parents.

Studies by Agras (1959) suggest that teachers were frequently not aware of the underlying depression in their failing students; or if they were aware, they did not seem to associate it with the chaotic conditions in the broken homes from which the students came. Nevertheless, when these students were afforded the opportunity, they could verbalize the feelings of rejection, futility, guilt, hostility, and low self-esteem that made up their depression. When their feelings and attitudes were recognized and treated appropriately, much of their unhappiness subsided, and their school work improved markedly. Sensitive and accepting adults can be of tremendous help to troubled children from broken homes if they will listen to them and try to understand their feelings and points of view.

Unfortunately this does not always work either. Many variables are involved in these types of emotional problems. Such factors as the age of the child at the time the home was broken and the attitude of the parent of the same sex make a marked difference in a child's ability to relate with that parent. Helping a child find a good parent surrogate with which to identify, such as a relative, a scoutmaster, a teacher, can be a great asset in developing in him a sound psychosexual identity.

The great lesson that I have learned over the past twenty years, working as a psychologist, is that the emotional problems stemming from broken homes are difficult and in many cases impossible to cure. Prevention, however, is relatively simple. It is to be found in a home where a strong father is firm but not harsh in the discipline of his children. At the same time he is also kind and considerate of his children's feelings and their attitudes that might be different from his own. This man loves his wife and children and is not ashamed to openly express his feelings of affection for all the members of his household. From this good father the children learn to appreciate and respect authority which they, of necessity, will have to live with all their lives. In this home there is also a gracious, empathetic mother who, also, is kind and considerate, who knows what it means to give of herself to her husband and children and yet does not feel imposed upon when called to make sacrifices for her family. She too loves her husband and children and feels comfortable in openly expressing her affection in the presence of all her family members. From this good mother the children develop self-esteem and feelings of adequacy to cope with life's problems. They also learn to become happy and secure individuals who are able to respect and love themselves as well as all persons with whom they come in contact. From both parents, then, comes that magic ingredient called *family solidarity*, which is so vital and necessary in the development of a happy home.

Yet, although the formula for the prevention of emotional problems is relatively simple, being a good father or mother is anything but simple or easy. It is hard, taxing labor that requires a lifetime of conscientious effort. Nevertheless, the rewards of healthy, well-adjusted, secure children are certainly worth all the time and energy put forth by parents for and in behalf of their family.

I am convinced that all the hospitals, clinics, medications, therapies, programs, philosophies, theories, and mental health movements in the world will never replace the home with good parents who love their children and are able to teach and train their offspring, through precept and example, the principles of sound mental health. Peace of mind, adequacy, and security must be taught in the home by parents during the children's early years of life or these crucial traits and characteristics will likely elude the individual throughout mortality. When Wordsworth said that the child is father to the man, he uttered a basic fact of life. What we learn as children from our parents will have tremendous influence on our behavior all the days of our lives.

Is divorce really the answer? Wouldn't a wiser solution to marital problems be for each mate to learn to become a better husband and father or a better wife and mother? As a counselor, you should remember to ask these questions of couples who come to you for help in saving their marriages.

References

Agras, Stewart. "The Relationship of School Phobia to Childhood Depression." American Journal of Psychiatry 116 (1959):533–36.

Publicover, Robert G. "The School and the Culturally Disadvantaged." *University of Utah Special Educator* 1 (1965):14–18.

Selected Readings

Bettleheim, Bruno. *Truants from Life: The Rehabilitation of Emotionally Disturbed Children.* Glencoe, Illinois: Free Press, 1955.

Faux, Eugene J. "Latency Age Children in a State Mental Hospital." *Provo Papers*, Winter, 1973.

Faux, Eugene J., and Rowley, C. M. "Detecting Depression in Childhood." *Hospital and Community Psychiatry*, Feb. 1967.

Jones, Ernest. *The Life and Work of Sigmund Freud.* New York: Basic Books, 1957.

About the Author

Experiences as an Army chaplain during the years 1952 through 1955 influenced Ben F. Mortensen to return to Brigham Young University, his alma mater, to begin his education toward a Ph.D. degree in clinical and counseling psychology. Awarded the United States Silver Star Medal for gallantry in action in Korea and the Korean Chung-Mu medal for bravery and meritorious service, Mortensen had witnessed psychotic breakdowns among the troops he counseled in Korea.

One soldier became hysterically blind upon witnessing the burning up of a buddy by a white phosphorous incendiary bomb. No physical damage had caused the soldier's blindness; it had been a defense mechanism, allowing him to blot out that scene and further scenes of horror. Mortensen saw other members of his outfit afflicted with "glove paralysis"—a hand paralyzed to the wrist instead of to the brain as in normal paralysis—a hysterical conversion reaction enabling a soldier to avoid firing a gun again. He saw a soldier afflicted with aphonia, or mutism—an inability to speak—a psychological mechanism resulting from battle fear unconsciously designed to remove him from the front lines.

The experience that really convinced him to take up counseling happened one morning on the front lines in Korea. A young soldier appeared at his bunker with a loaded rifle, declaring to his chaplain (Mortensen) that he wanted to commit suicide but didn't have a good reason for doing so. He had mulled over his predicament all night, finally deciding he would kill the chaplain (nice fellow that he was); that would give him ample reason for taking his own life. Several hours later Mortensen finally convinced this young soldier that his decision was a bad one.

In 1960 Mortensen was awarded the Doctor of Philosophy degree in clinical and counseling psychology at the University of Utah. During his internship at the VA Hospital in Salt Lake City, he had a rewarding experience. He had been assigned to a WAC who had suffered a psychotic breakdown and who had not spoken for three years. After six months of reading to her, talking to her, and singing to her, he said, "Virginia, you're making me look bad. I've tried everything I know to help you, and you haven't even so much as looked at me. Please, won't you say just one word? If you don't, the psychiatrist will have to give you more electro-shock therapy." He was rendered speechless at her response: "Dr. Mortensen, if you let them do that to me, I'll never speak to you again!" From that moment she rapidly improved. She was discharged not long after that and began to work as a secretary in Salt Lake City.

Dr. Mortensen is now employed as a clinical psychologist at the Utah State Hospital in Provo, Utah. He and his wife, the former Rene Rhead, have six children and four grandchildren—all preserved for posterity on the dedication page of this book.

Brigham Young University Press, a member of the
American Association of University Presses, shares
fully the AAUP dedication to excellence in university
press publishing.

At BYU Press we focus mainly—but not solely—on
Western regional studies and early childhood
education.

Authors with manuscripts in these and related areas
may submit queries to Managing Editor, BYU press,
218 UPB, Brigham Young University, Provo, UT
84602, USA.